BECOMING
DEEPLY ROOTED IN YOUR
Faith

TINA YOUNG

ISBN 978-1-0980-2610-3 (paperback)
ISBN 978-1-0980-2611-0 (digital)

Christian Faith Publishing, Inc.
832 Park Avenue
Meadville, PA 16335
www.christianfaithpublishing.com

Printed in the United States of America

CONTENTS

INTRODUCTION

My dear precious ones, God wants more in your life than you could ever imagine. His thoughts toward you are pure. His love for you is deeper than the ocean and is wider than the east is from the west. He has a plan and a purpose for your life. He knew you before you were born and has your days numbered. I want to encourage you that you didn't choose this book for no reason; God knew you would be reading this book. Life is not by chance or by coincidence. Everything has a purpose and a reason why it happens. As you work your way through this study workbook, I know that God will meet you right where you are. This book is designed for all stages of life's walk with Christ.

* For those who don't know Christ in a personal way, by the end of this study workbook, my prayer is you will.
* For those who do and are wanting to grow deeper, this study workbook will take you as deep as you will allow.
* For those who have become stagnate or is struggling with life challenges, this study workbook will refresh you and give you the hope you need to press on.

I know He will meet you because He met me in all levels of my relationship with Him. He never leaves us nor forsake us. He doesn't have favorites. He loves us all equally. Now open your heart and mind to the Holy Spirit and let Him guide you through this study workbook. Before you start the study pray this prayer aloud: "Father God, I come before You and I humble myself. I ask You Holy Spirit to awake me and bring the words of the Holy Bible alive in me. Open my mind to understand what I'm reading. Make it come alive in my spirit, help me to apply it to my life. In Jesus name I pray Amen."

HOW TO USE THIS BOOK

Please use this book in the way it most suits you. If the best way for you to grow deeper in your relationship with Christ is with other people do that. If you are one who grows deeper alone do that. But I will encourage you to develop a few close friends who you can really trust to hold you accountable. It is very helpful in times of trouble or in times of doubting; to have someone you can lean on and to share your thoughts with to be like Jesus in the flesh for you.

As you go through each section you will find scriptures and references to help you study out what the scripture's truth are. There are websites you can use to look up scripture. BibleGateway.com or BlueLetterBible.com, these two websites lets you type in a phrase to find scriptures. Sometimes you need to reword the phrase or just put in one word in the search bar. As the list of scriptures pulls up, you read them until one of them speaks to your heart. This will be the one God wants you to study and learn from. Read that scripture in several versions to get a fuller understanding. Write this scripture out and refer to it until you have it settled in your heart. Bible Gateway and Blue Letter Bible have study tools that you can access and read to get a better understanding of what the scriptures is saying. It gives insight into the culture and time period. It helps you to understand how to apply it to your life.

websterdictionary1828.com is another resource I use to study the meanings of words, so I can get a fuller understanding of the word. Sometimes the word I'm studying has scripture references, so then you can see others places in the Bible it is used, and this will build your knowledge. And if you allow it to touch your heart, it will bring a new level of trusting God in new areas of your life.

* There will be questions that will help you compare your thoughts to the words you read in the Bible to bring a better understanding of your thought life. This practice will help you align your thoughts to the Word of God written in the Holy Bible.
* You will write out a pray confessing these truths in your life. This step will help develop hope and build trust in God for everything.
* Learning to trust God is vital to our growth. We need to know how to lean on Him during the hard times and to release all your cares and worries onto Jesus Christ, our redeemer.

To honor Him with your praises as He blesses, strengthens, encourages or carries you through a hard time, to show Him your thankfulness for what He has done already, and to give thanks for what He is going to do.

* I will share personal testimony on how the Holy Bible's truths is a live and active in my life.

Father God, I lift each one who reads and does this study workbook to You. I pray God that You meet each one right where they are. That Your Words from the Holy Bible builds them up and places them on a firm foundation, so they cannot be shaken. As it is stated in Psalms 125: "Those who trust in the Lord are like Mount Zion, which cannot be shaken but endures forever." God, I ask You to anoint each person with Your Holy Spirit; open their heart and mind to Your Word; open their ability to understand, so they can walk in Your truth; pour Your endless love over them, for Your perfect love casts out fear; heal any brokenness in their life; give them the eyes to see who You have created them to be; prepare them to receive all You have and want for them; reveal Yourself to them in a very personal way; protect their mind from the thoughts that keep them captive; help them to find friends that they can trust, that will encourage, and stand with them without judging but instead loving them with Your unconditional love; guide them in this study to get the most out of it; and allow them to see the changes You desire them to make, which will bring them into a deeper relationship with You. I pray this in Jesus's name. Amen.

Section 1

Hearing the Voice of the Lord

Every king in all the earth shall give You thanks, O Lord, for all of them shall hear Your voice.

—Psalm 138:4TLB

As life continues to move at its fast pace, we feel we never have time to stop and just rest. To take time to recover seem impossible. We are faced with choices that need to be made daily; sometimes they need to be made in an instance. We all need to ask ourselves these questions, do we make these choices on our own or with the influence of family and friends, or do we seek God? What voice is the loudest in your life, yours, the world's, or God's? When we can truthfully answer these two questions about ourselves, then we can make the adjustments that is needed to be made, which is to be a hearer of God's voice.

Sometimes we doubt whether we can hear from the Lord or whether we hear Him correctly. As we study the scriptures, the scripture will give us a better understanding and develop our trust and build our confidence for our heavenly Father, the Holy Spirit, and Jesus Christ. There are times we hear Him and choose not to obey. When this happens, we will face the consequences of our disobedience.

Zephaniah 3:2 The Living Bible (TLB): "In her pride she won't listen even to the voice of God. No one can tell her anything; she refuses all correction. She does not trust the Lord nor seek for God."

What attitude is active within her? _____. She won't _____. She _____ all _____. She does not_____ Who _____. She won't _____ for _____.

Exodus 15:26 TLB: "If you will listen to the voice of the Lord your God, and obey it, and do what is right, then I will not make you suffer the diseases I sent on the Egyptians, for I am the Lord who heals you."

If we _____ to the _____ of the _____. What do we need to do _____ and do what is _____? What will the Lord do for you? I won't make you_____ the _____. He wants to _____ you.

Psalm 138:4 TLB: "Every king in all the earth shall give You thanks, O Lord, for all of them shall hear Your voice."

What are we to give to the Lord? _____. Who shall hear His voice? _____. That means you and I can hear His voice if we will be thankful and still our self long enough to listen.

His voice can be as soft as a whisper.

Job 26:14 Good News Translation (GNT): "But these are only hints of His power, only the whispers that we have heard. Who can know how truly great God is?"

What do we get hints of _____? We can hear only the _____. He can be loud and thundering.

Psalm 29:3 TLB: "The voice of the Lord echoes from the clouds. The God of glory thunders through the skies."

What does God voice do from the clouds? _____. Who thunders through the sky? _____ of _____. His voice can be a cry from the wilderness when we are lost and wandering in our ways.

Luke 3:4 TLB: "In the words of Isaiah the prophet, John was a voice shouting from the barren wilderness, 'Prepare a road for The Lord to travel on! Widen the pathway before Him!'"

Who was the voice shouting? _____where was he shouting from? _____. What was he asking for us to do? _____ a _____ Who are we to prepare it for? _____ what are we to do with the path? _____. Sometimes, He will use other people to speak into our lives. Like He used John the Baptist and other prophets in the Old Testaments. He is the fire that burns within our spirit, like the fire that draws the children of Israel.

Deuteronomy 5:23–26 New International Version (NIV):

When you heard the voice out of the darkness, while the mountain was ablaze with fire, all the leaders of your tribes and your elders came to me. And you said, "The LORD our God has shown us His glory and His majesty, and we have heard His voice from the fire. Today we have seen that a person can live even if God speaks with them. But now, why should we die? This great fire will consume us, and we will die if we hear the voice of the LORD our God any longer. For what mortal has ever heard the voice of the living God speaking out of fire, as we have, and survived? Go near and listen to all that the LORD our God says. Then tell us whatever the LORD our God tells you. We will listen and obey."

How did God present himself? A mountain_____ with _____. What had He shown? His _____ and His _____. What did the people express? We _____ His _____. What did the living God do with His people? He_____ to them. What did the people ask Moses to do on their behalf? Go _____ and _____ to all. What were the people willing to do? _____ and _____.

So if the children of Israel could hear His voice and God's promises are true to this day. This reassures us that we can hear His voice. What we need to do is willing go near to Him and seek Him. We need to be willing to listen and obey what we hear from Him. These scriptures have shown us that He can speak directly to us in a small still or loud voice through His Word or through other people. Let us keep our ears and heart open to the voice of the Lord.

Jude 1:20 New International Reader's Version (NIRV): "Dear friends, build yourselves up in your most Holy Faith. Let the Holy Spirit guide and help you when you pray."

What are we to do? _____ yourself _____. How with _____. Who is the guide? The _____.

1 John 5:6–8 TLB:

> And we know He is, because God said so with a voice from heaven when Jesus was baptized, and again as He was facing death yes, not only at His baptism but also as He faced death.* And the Holy Spirit, forever truthful, says it too. So we have these three witnesses: the voice of the Holy Spirit in our hearts, the voice from heaven at Christ's baptism, and the voice before He died.* And they all say the same thing: that Jesus Christ is the Son of God.

Where did the voice come from? _____
Whose voice was it? _____. Who speaks truthfully? The
_____. Where does that voice reside?
_____. How many witnesses? _____. To whom
do the two voices belong? _____ and the
_____ from _____. Who were the voices
witnessing about? _____? So we are to let the
Holy Spirit guide us during our prayer times, by doing this we build
ourselves up in faith.

Faith comes by hearing the Word of God.

Romans 10:17 NIV: "Consequently, faith comes from hearing the message, and the message is heard through the Word about Christ."

The Holy Spirit only guides us with truth, so if what you are praying about doesn't line up with the scriptures it most likely is our own spirit trying to guide us. We are made up a three part being: spirit, soul, and body

First Thessalonians 5:23 NIV: "May God Himself, the God of peace, sanctify you through and through. May your whole spirit, soul and body be kept blameless at the coming of our Lord Jesus Christ."

John 5:7 Amplified Bible (AMP): "So there are three witnesses in heaven: the Father, the Word, and the Holy Spirit, and these three are One."

John 16:13 AMP: "But when He, the Spirit of Truth (the truth-giving Spirit) comes, He will guide you into all the truth (the whole, full truth). For He will not speak His own message [on His own authority]; but He will tell whatever He hears [from the Father; He will give the message that has been given to Him], and He will announce and declare to you the things that are to come [that will happen in the future]."

Who comes _____ of _____. What does He do _____ us in all _____? Whose message does He give? _____. He declares our _____.

Romans 8:15–16 NIV: "The Spirit you received does not make you slaves, so that you live in fear again; rather, the Spirit you received brought about your adoption to sonship. And by Him we cry, 'Abba, Father.' The Spirit Himself testifies with our spirit that we are God's children."

What did we receive? The _____. This Spirit doesn't make us _____ or to live in _____. We are _____ into _____. We are children of _____.

John 10:4 NIV: "When He has brought out all His own, He goes on ahead of them, and His sheep follow Him because they know His voice."

Pray this prayer aloud: Father God, anoint our ears, so we can hear and know without any doubt that we know Your voice. Holy Spirit we understand it is Your job to guide us in the way we should go to declare our future, to reveal the truth in order to bring us into understanding of who we are and what we are created for. Open our heart as You guide our reading the Word of God. Amen

I want to share a few examples from my own personal walk with Lord on how His voice has been revealed to me. This study workbook is a result of me being willing to go and seek the Lord and obey what He said. A precious woman of God came to me in August 2013. She felt that the Lord had put it on her heart to talk to me about leading a Bible study with some women in our church. She was thinking something on marriage; she even gave me a book to read and asked me to seek God's direction. Leading a study was not anything I had done before; it had never really crossed my mind. So I took the request to God. I started to read the book, so I could get an idea if this is what I should do. This was not something I took lightly or felt I should rush into. I spent about a month listening and trusting that I was hearing from God correctly.

Early one Saturday morning, I was awakened by God. I heard Him so clearly telling me, "Yes, I am to lead a study but not on marriage." He spoke to me about "My people don't know My love or who I really Am." He gave me these key points to focus the study around.

* How do I know the voice of the Lord? This question builds our confidence that God really does speak to us and show us how He does, and we can trust that small, still voice.

* Who does God say I am? With this question, we discover who we are in Christ and replace our thoughts of who we think we are with what God declares. It brings healing and restores us to become who we were created to be.

* Who does God say He is? With all the earthly experiences we live out we have a distorted image of who God really is. This question helps us to replace how we see God.

* What are God's promises? We get to discover that His promises are true and active in our lives. As we allow the Holy Spirit to guide us in our reading time of the Holy Bible, the promises will come alive in us. As we cling to His promises in the Word of God, we find the strength needed to climb to the mountaintop in victory or make it out of the valley of death safely.

* What did Jesus do for me? With this question, we can discover salvation, healing, comfort, peace, sanctification, mercy, grace. He is our advocate and so much more.

The second example was in 2010. The Lord started to whisper to my heart that change was coming, and He put this desire to check out a different church, which was closer to where I lived. My family was, at that time, attending a church that was thirty-five minutes away and the drive was getting to me. I would push the thought of switching churches away for fear that it was my own desire. Finally, I started to pray about it, asking the Lord, "If You really wants us to change churches, You need to speak it to my husband's heart. I will obey You when he tells me that You have been talking to him about changing churches."

Every time that thought came, I watered it in prayer. In October 2012, right before my husband John was leaving to go on a hunting trip to Colorado, he said to me, "Honey, I must tell you something and it may sound strange, but I know it is from God." God has been talking to me for the past two years that we need to check out Cornerstone Church in Litchfield. "He said that we need to be more connected to our community." I responded with such excitement. I said to John, "God does talk to you and you listen." Then I told him "that God has been talking to me for about two years about changing churches, also I had been praying to God to make it clear to you, and when you tell me I will obey."

I want you all to realize that God's timing is perfect, that He will start speaking to you about change coming and preparing you for it. Our part is to be a hear and a doer of His commands. My third example is in 2011 on October 6th our son Kevin was killed in a car accident. We were still apart of the Hutchinson church body. I was an example to a lady who lost her son the end of September 2012 in a car accident. I got the opportunity to share with her God's faithfulness to my family, and how He brought me through the death of my Son. In beginning of 2013 we were attending a church in Litchfield. I had the opportunity again to love on a family who son was killed in a car accident on September 30th 2013. By our obedience in waiting for God's timing I was able to love on both families sharing God's faithfulness and His love with them. I shared with them "joy can surround you in the time of grief and God brings good out of the depths of our grief."

Mark 12:20 The Message (MSG): "But the seed planted in the good earth represents those who hear the Word, embrace it, and produce a harvest beyond their wildest dreams."

What does good earth represent? _____ the _____. What is our responsibility? _____ it. When we do our part what happens? _____ a _____. When we are willing do our part, God will complete His part.

Now I want you to take some time and allow the Holy Spirit to guide you in your reading time. Find one passage of scripture that awakens inside of you. Write it down with the scripture's address and the version of the Bible. Next, answer these questions about that scripture passage. What is it about this scripture that spoke to you? Do you truly believe what it says? Yes or no. In your own words explain your reason on why you believe or don't. Answering these questions will tell you about your heart's condition, and the Holy Spirit will bring change if it is needed. How will I apply this truth to my life?

Ask the Holy Spirit to reveal to you if you have walked this scripture out in your life and write it out? This will show you how God has been working in your life and build your testimony to share with others. Next write out a prayer confessing this scripture. If you believe what the scripture says, start your prayer with Lord I believe Your Word. If you don't believe yet, start your prayer with Lord help me to believe what Your Word says, I want to believe Your Word and the promises it has for me. As you learn to confess the Word of God over your life you will see circumstances begin to change. You will begin to see who God has created you to be.

Genesis 9:6–7 MSG: "Whoever sheds human blood, by humans let his blood be shed, because God made humans in His Image reflecting God's very nature. You're here to bear fruit, reproduce, lavish life on the earth, live bountifully!"

Who Made Humans? _____ Whose image are we made in? _____. Whose nature are we to reflect? _____ Why are we here? _____, lavish life on earth and _____!

Do this lesson five times to build your knowledge and trust in God's Word. If you want to go deeper, find corresponding scriptures and look up words whose meanings you are unsure of. You may want to purchase a Bible dictionary, or if you have a very old dictionary, that will work also. Or you can go to Websterdictonary1828.com. Don't be in a rush to get to the next section. If this takes you a week or a month, it is okay. Heart transformations comes from our diligence to allow God's Word to transform us.

Here is an example of what your study will look like; it doesn't need to be exactly like mine. Allow the Holy Spirit room to work.

Scripture

Jude 1:20–21 NLT: "But you dear friend, must build each other up in your most holy faith, pray in the power of the Holy Spirit. And await the mercy of our Lord Jesus Christ, who will bring you eternal life. In this way you keep yourselves safe in God's love."

What is it about this scripture that spoke to you? To build others up is to speak the Word of God over them and praying for them. My faith is built up by hearing the Word. The Holy Spirit gives power to my prayers and helps me pray. I must trust and wait and allow God's mercy to perform in my life. As I walk this out, I keep myself safe in God's love. When I am safe in God's love, there is no room for doubt. I will know I'm doing His will.

Do you truly believe what it says? Yes

How will I apply this truth to my life? By taking time to pray for others and myself daily, asking the Holy Spirit to show me how to pray, and trusting that God will help complete the work. I know that God has been working through my prayers. He has brought attitude changes in me and is creating me into His image. I used to think I wasn't a loveable person, that I wasn't wanted. I didn't like who I was or what I thought about myself. I had believed the lies Satan had spoken to me through others. But by taking time to do this study, I learned whose image I was created to be like. God is making my life complete when I placed all the pieces before Him. When I repented of my sins, He gave me a fresh start.

Indeed, I've kept alert to God's ways; I haven't taken God for granted. Every day, I review the ways He works. I try not to miss a trick. I feel put back together, and I'm watching my step. God rewrote the text of my life when I opened the book of my heart to His eyes. He will do the same for you because we are all equal in His eyes.

Prayer

> Father God, I do believe that praying in the power of the Holy Spirit will build up my holy faith, that He will guide my prayers, so I can build others up. Holy Spirit, give me the patience to wait, fill me with the mercy of the Lord Jesus Christ, and help me stay focused on eternal life. Father God, thank You for keeping me safe in Your love. In Jesus's name, I pray. Amen.

Scripture

Psalm 25: 8:10 NLT: "The Lord is good and does what is right; He shows the proper path to those who go astray. He leads the humble in doing right; teaching them His way. The Lord leads with unfailing love and faithfulness all who keep His covenant and obey His demands."

What is it about this scripture that spoke to you? When I stray, He will show me the proper path. It gives me a great sense of confidence that He will guide me when I stay humble toward Him. This teaches me a way to have peace through all the events that occurred in my life.

Do you truly believe what it says? Yes

I do believe because I know that God keeps His promises. He is faithful. I know that, for this promise to be active, I need to do my part and be humble before the Lord. To do this, I need to use my faith and trust in God fully.

Journal and Note Page

Proper—suitable, right, fit; conforming to the best usage.

Humble—not proud or assertive; Not pretentious.

Astray—out of right way, wrong.

Paraphrased Psalm 25:8–10 TLB: The Lord is good and glad to teach the proper path to all who go astray. He will teach the ways that are right and best to those who humbly turn to Him, every path He guides us on is fragrant with His loving kindness and His truth.

Psalm 32:8–11 New King James Version (NKJV): "I will instruct you and teach you in the way you should go; I will guide you with My eye."

There will be times we will break God's commands. When we do this, if we are sincere in our repentance and cling to God with our faith, in complete awe of His majesty, and worship Him with reverence, God will instruct and direct our ways. We are all sinners, and God's desire is to teach us the way of reconciliation with Him. The way to a well-grounded peace and eternal life is through accepting Jesus Christ as your personal savior. His gospel, makes this way known to all, and with His spirit, opening an understanding. We need to take action to desire it. The devil leads men blindfolded to hell; but God enlightens men's eyes, sets things before them in true light, and so leads them to heaven. If we remain meek, He will teach us. In our own eyes, we need to remain humble. He will teach sinners with wisdom, tenderness, and compassion, and as much as they are able to bear. He will teach them His ways; we need to desire to be taught that and to choose the right way. He, who directed our choice, will direct our steps and will lead us in it. If we choose wisely, God will give us grace to walk wisely. God will make us at easy. The soul that is sanctified by the grace of God and much more, that is comforted by the peace of God dwells at ease. Even when the body is sick and lies in pain, it may dwell at ease in God. He calls them not servants, but friends; God gives His counsel in close friendships.

Scripture:

_____
_____
_____
_____
_____
_____

What is it about this scripture that spoke to you

_____
_____
_____
_____
_____
_____

Do you truly believe what it says? Yes or no. Explain your answer.

_____
_____
_____
_____
_____
_____

Journal Page

_____
_____
_____
_____
_____
_____
_____
_____
_____
_____
_____
_____
_____
_____
_____
_____
_____
_____
_____
_____
_____
_____
_____
_____
_____
_____
_____
_____
_____

How will I apply this truth to my life?

_____
_____
_____
_____
_____
_____

Write out your prayer:

_____
_____
_____
_____
_____
_____

If the Holy Spirit has revealed a time, you have lived this truth out. Write it down.

_____
_____
_____
_____
_____
_____

Scripture:

_____
_____
_____
_____
_____
_____

What is it about this scripture that spoke to you?

_____

_____

_____

_____

_____

_____

Do you truly believe what it says? Yes or no. Explain your answer.

_____

_____

_____

_____

_____

_____

Journal Page

_____
_____
_____
_____
_____
_____
_____
_____
_____
_____
_____
_____
_____
_____
_____
_____
_____
_____
_____
_____
_____
_____
_____
_____
_____
_____
_____
_____
_____
_____

How will I apply this truth to my life?

_____
_____
_____
_____
_____
_____

Write out your prayer:

_____
_____
_____
_____
_____

If the Holy Spirit has revealed a time, you have lived this truth out. Write it down.

_____
_____
_____
_____
_____

Scripture:

_____
_____
_____
_____
_____

What is it about this scripture that spoke to you?

_____

_____

_____

_____

_____

_____

Do you truly believe what it says? Yes or no. Explain your answer.

_____

_____

_____

_____

_____

_____

Journal Page

_____
_____
_____
_____
_____
_____
_____
_____
_____
_____
_____
_____
_____
_____
_____
_____
_____
_____
_____
_____
_____
_____
_____
_____
_____
_____
_____
_____
_____
_____
_____
_____
_____
_____
_____

How will I apply this truth to my life?

_____

_____

_____

_____

_____

_____

Write out your prayer:

_____

_____

_____

_____

_____

_____

If the Holy Spirit has revealed a time, you have lived this truth out. Write it down.

_____

_____

_____

_____

_____

Scripture:

_____

_____

_____

_____

_____

What is it about this scripture that spoke to you?

_____

_____

_____

_____

_____

_____

Do you truly believe what it says? Yes or no. Explain your answer.

_____

_____

_____

_____

_____

_____

Journal Page

How will I apply this truth to my life?

_____
_____
_____
_____
_____
_____

Write out your prayer:

_____
_____
_____
_____
_____

If the Holy Spirit has revealed a time, you have lived this truth out. Write it down.

_____
_____
_____
_____
_____
_____

Scripture:

_____
_____
_____
_____
_____

What is it about this scripture that spoke to you?

_____
_____
_____
_____
_____
_____

Do you truly believe what it says? Yes or no. Explain your answer.

_____
_____
_____
_____
_____
_____

Journal Page

_____

_____

_____

_____

_____

_____

_____

_____

_____

_____

_____

_____

_____

_____

_____

_____

_____

_____

_____

_____

_____

_____

_____

_____

_____

_____

_____

_____

_____

_____

_____

How will I apply this truth to my life?

_____

_____

_____

_____

_____

_____

Write out your prayer:

_____

_____

_____

_____

_____

If the Holy Spirit has revealed a time, you have lived this truth out. Write it down.

_____

_____

_____

_____

_____

Section 2

Who God Says I Am

So, you are complete through the union with Christ, who is head over every ruler and authority.

—Colossians 2:10 NLT

Have these questions ever run through your mind? I know these questions have plagued my mind for years:

- You don't know who you are?
- You don't like who you are?
- Why are we here on earth?
- Why am I the way I am?

In this section of the workbook, you will discover the answers to these questions. As you study the Bible deeper, you will discover who you are and why you are here on the earth. You will discover the gifts and talents God formed inside you. As you study the scriptures, they will renew your mind to the Word of God, and it will set you free from the deception that you once lived in.

As we travel the road of life, we encounter many adversities in life that try to mold and shape us into who we are to be. Ask yourself what mirror you are looking in. Is the mirror the world's view, which are your friends', coworkers', or Hollywood's? Is the mirror of your loved ones—your parents/grandparents, siblings, husband, boyfriend/girlfriend, or your kids? or is your mirror God's? We all use each mirror at different times in our life; what we need to learn is only take a glimpse in the world's and our loved one's mirrors and gaze into God's mirror.

How do we gaze into God's mirror? By reading of His Word and studying it out and applying it to our lives. We cannot just be a hearer of the Word we need to be a doer for a real change, a godly change to come.

Ask yourself, Do I want to change? Do I want to be all God wants me to be?

Once this is settled in your heart, you will become the doer and apply the Word of God to your life, and you will see changes starting to take place. You are a work in progress. As long as you have breath and the desire to be like Christ, you will be changed day by day, week by week, month by month, year by year until you meet your creator face to face.

Pray this prayer aloud: Holy Father God, I glorify You as my creator. You are my author and finisher. I know what You have started in me You will finish. I ask You, Holy Spirit, keep my heart soft and open to the Word of God. Open my ears to hear Your voice as I open the Word of God, reveal Your Word to me; give me the understanding I need to apply the Word to my life. Give me the courage to face the mirrors in my life and learn to just glimpse at the ones that give me a distorted view of myself and to turn to Your mirror and gaze, which gives me a complete, accurate view of who I am. In Jesus's name, I pray. Amen.

Let's begin to gaze into God's Word and see how He see your reflection in the mirror. So you can see the changes needed so, you become an accurate reflection of who God created you to be.

Psalms 89:13 MSG:

> Oh yes, You shaped me first inside, then out; You formed me in my mother's womb. I thank You, High God You're breathtaking! Body and soul, I am marvelously made! I worship in adoration what a creation! You know me inside and out, You know every bone in my body; You know exactly how I was made, bit by bit, how I was sculpted from nothing into something. Like an open book, You watched me grow from conception to birth; all the stages of my life were spread out before You, the days of my life all prepared before I'd even lived one day.

God knows us very intimately. He knows every detail about us, our every fault, and every attribute of goodness. He knows all our choices before we even need to make one. He knows when we will choose to obey or disobey in every situation. He knows the right person for you and me to marry, what job is the best for us. He knows who our best friends will be.

Are you seeking Him for direction in your life? I can say yes at times. I have, and there are times I haven't. At an early age, if we haven't been introduced or taught to seek God, we won't understand the importance of seeking Him. We live our life blindly under the influence of Satan. God created us for a relationship with Him.

Are we allowing our family and friends be the main influences for the choices we make? The influences of others can direct our choices toward God while others take us down the wrong path away from God. Without any doubt, I have chosen the wrong path when I chose to have sex outside of marriage before I met John. I had been told that it was a sin, but I didn't have the understanding or the heart commitment to obey what God clearly speaks about this because I hadn't study it and nor lived this lifestyle.

Hebrews 13:4 AMP: "Marriage *is to be held* in honor among all [that is, regarded as something of great value], and the *marriage* bed undefiled [by immorality or by any sexual sin]; for God will judge the sexually immoral and adulterous."

Making this choice of allowing the influence of my boyfriend to persuade me had a huge effect on my marriage to John for many years. It was very difficult for me to enjoy the fullness of being intimate. My action made John feel rejected and inadequate. I had to confess my sin to God, myself, and to John. I had to ask for forgiveness from God, myself, and John before a healing in me could take place so our intimacy could be blessed and be fulfilling.

Jeremiah 1:5 TLB: "I knew you before you were formed within your mother's womb; before you were born, I sanctified you and appointed you as My spokesman to the world."

God knew us before we were formed in our mother's _____. He _____ us and _____ us to be a _____ to the world.

Are you seeing what I'm seeing? God knew us before we were formed in our mother's womb. He knew who our mother and father were going to be before they were even created. He has everything under control. He knows exactly who needs to be in our lives to help mold and shape us into who He wants us to be. God declares we are sanctified, which means dedicated and consecrated. Let's look deeper into the word "sanctify." What is sanctify? To set apart as holy. To make free from sin. So before He formed us, He set us apart and made us free from sin. So when our sinful nature rises in us and we sin, all we need to do is confess the sin to God and repent, which is to turn from the sin. He created away for us to live a life dedicated to Him. He longs for us to be in a relationship with Him. Through this relationship, we can trust Him fully and declare His goodness by living a life that glorifies Him.

Nehemiah 9:5–6 MSG: "Blessed be Your glorious name, exalted above all blessing and praise! You're the One, God, You made the heavens, and the heavens of heavens, and all the angles: the earth and everything on it, the seas and everything in them; You keep them all alive; heaven's angels worship You!"

Who made the heavens, the earth, the sea, and everything in them? _____. So if He created everything, including you, doesn't He deserve praise, worship, and thanksgiving? Let us take time now to thank Him.

Pray this prayer aloud: Holy God, You are the creator of all thing, including me. You are perfect in all You do. As I see all the beauty in the creation You have created, I know You have created beauty in me also. With each breath I take, I want to give You honor and glory. Lord, at times my eyes go astray or wander from You, and I become distracted and focused on the circumstances around me. I ask You to forgive me, Lord. I surrender my heart and life fully to You right now. I ask that You refresh me in Your glorious presence. I purposely turn my eyes back to You, oh God. I declare my love for You, Lord Jesus Christ. I thank You for all You did for me on the cross, how You paid the price for my life, so I can have eternal life with our heavenly Father God. In Jesus's name, I pray. Amen.

First Corinthians 3:16 MSG: "You realize, don't you, that you are the temple of God, and God Himself is present in you? No one will get by with vandalizing God's temple, you can be sure of that. God's temple is sacred—and you, remember, *are* the temple."

What does this scripture declare you are? _____
_____. Who resides in you? _____. God's temple is _____. We are the temple of God.

God resides in us when we accepted Him as our Lord and savior. Have you done this? If not, ask yourself why.

If you haven't yet, it is okay to continue with this study; it will guide you on the importance of accepting Jesus as your savior and His residing in you.

As we read earlier in Jeremiah 1:5, God appoints us as His spokesperson to the world. We are to declare His goodness, His love and mercy to others.

Deuteronomy 18:12 MSG: "So now Israel, what do you think God expects from you? Just this live in His presence in holy reverence, follow the road He sets out for you, love Him, serve God, your God with everything you have in you, obey the commandments and regulations of God that I'm commanding you today—live a good life."

Have you ever wondered what a relationship with someone you can't see looks like? I know I did. Any relationship takes communication, time, dedication, and serving one another. So how do we have a relationship with our creator? We spend time reading the Bible, His Word. We communicate by talking to Him in regular conversation, as you would with people. The second part of communication is listening. Listening can be the hardest part because we live in a time where we expect instant responses. Sometimes, God is not instant but speaks through His Word or through another person. So if you don't hear something instantly, keep seeking Him throughout your day through small conversations. This is where we can learn to be patient by practicing listening. Whatever we are dedicated to, we will take the time for. So ask yourself, Am I dedicated to God and His plan for my life? Do I show Him reverence? Let's look at what reverence means. It is a feeling or attitude of deep respect or love and awe, as for something sacred. So if we have an attitude of deep respect, we would honor God with our words and actions, which means we would obey His commands and His plan for our life.

So how do we serve someone we cannot see? By sharing the goodness of God, His love for others, extending His mercy and kindness. We can do this by praying with others for their needs, sharing a scripture that gives them hope, or preparing a meal for someone who is sick or just lost a loved one. You can help with a project in the community that helps those in need. These are just a few ideas.

Communication also comes through worship.

Nehemiah 5:5 MSG: "Blessed be Your Glorious name, exalted above all blessing and praises! You're the One, God, You alone, You made the heavens, the heavens of heavens, and all angels; the earth and everything on it the seas and everything in them: You keep them alive; heaven's angels worship You!"

Worship is one of the highest forms of serving God.

Psalm 95:6–7 MSG: "So come, let us worship: bow before Him, on your knees before God, who made us! Oh yes, He's our God, and we're the people He pastures, the flock He feeds."

We are to come and do what? _____ and _____ before Him.

Who made us? _____. We declare that _____ is our _____. What does He do for us _____ the flock and _____ us. What an amazing God we have. Give Him thanks right now.

Oh, glories! God, I want to thank You with everything within me. You are gracious and good. Thank You for how You care for me and how You Love me so intensely. Thank You for all Your goodness. Your glory and strength You pour on me. I will praise You with my lips daily. Amen.

Romans 10:9–10 HCSB: "If you confess with your mouth, "Jesus is Lord", and believe in your heart that God raised Him from the dead, you will be saved. One believes with the heart, resulting in righteousness, and confess with the mouth, resulting in salvation."

These scriptures are key to your personal relationship with God. If you haven't done this yet, you may want to.

Pray this prayer aloud: Father God, I come before You and confess that I am a sinner and I need a savior. I believe that Your Son, Jesus Christ, died on the cross and rose from the dead for me. Jesus, I ask You to come into my life and be my Lord and Savior. I can't do life on my own. I need Your Holy Spirit to be my guide. Come into my life now. In Jesus Christ, I pray. Amen.

If you are not ready to pray this yet, that is okay. Continue with the study; it will help you understand why you would want to.

Malachi 3:17 Amplified Bible (AMP): "And they shall be Mine, says the Lord of hosts, in that day when I publicly recognize *and* openly declare them to be My jewels (My special possession, My peculiar treasure). And I will spare them, as a man spares his own son who serves him."

What does the Lord of hosts declare they shall be? _____.
He will _____ recognize and openly _____ them
as His _____, _____, _____.
My _____, My _____. He will _____
those who serve Him.

We are His special possession, a jewel, a treasure. He calls you mine. He will declare publicly that you belong to Him. Oh, how exciting is that. When you have something very special to you, you take great care of it. You want to show it off to all your family and friends. If we earthly humans do this, can you imagine how much more God wants to care for us and show us off? His love for us is so deep and unmeasurable. If you call God yours, He is your treasure. Do you share Him with others? Do you show His love, mercy, kindness, patience, and grace?

Ephesians 5:1–2 MSG: "Watch what God does, and then you do it, like children who learn proper behavior from their parents. Mostly what God does is love you. Keep company with Him and learn a life of love. Observe how Christ loved us. His love was not cautious but extravagant. He didn't love in order to get something from us but to give everything of Himself to us. Love like that."

Who are we to watch? _____. Then we _____
it. What mostly does God do _____.
How are we to learn what God does _____
with Him. Who are we to observe? _____ How is
Christ's love described? _____. He didn't love to get
_____ but to give _____ of _____
to us.

We are called to _____ like that. God declares you
are loved and loved extravagantly by His Son, Jesus Christ, and He
doesn't expect anything in return from us but does expect us to love
like that, unconditionally, toward Him, our family, friends, and even
coworkers and fellow believers and nonbelievers even those who irri-
tate, or violated us causing great emotional damage. Many of us at
times feel unloved. I know I have at times. When those feelings or
thoughts of doubt come over me, I need to replace them with what
God says, "I am loved." I need to walk in His kind of love, the love
that expects nothing back, extravagant love.

Pray this prayer aloud: Dear heavenly Father, I come humbly
before You to seek Your forgiveness for not accepting the extravagant
love You have for me through Your son, Jesus Christ. I ask that You
bestow Your love on me now as a cloak that completely covers me.
Father God, I ask that You forgive me for not always acting in Your
love toward others, especially toward my husband (put the name of
who the Holy Spirit reveals to you). Holy Spirit, I ask that You help
keep me humble and help me to understand the fullness of Your
extravagant love. In Jesus's name, I pray. Amen.

Genesis 1:26–28 Holman Christian Standard Bible (HCSB):

Then God said, "Let us make man in Our
image, according to Our likeness. they will rule
the fish of the sea, the birds of the sky, the live-
stock, all the earth, and the creatures that crawl
on earth." So God created man in His own image;
He created him in the image of God; He created
them male and female. God blessed them, and

God said to them, "be fruitful and multiply, fill the earth, and subdue it. Rule the fish of the sea, the birds of the sky, and every creature that crawls on the earth."

Genesis 1:31 MSG "God looked over everything He had made; it was so good, so very good! It was evening, it was morning."

Day 6

Who created man? _____. In whose image are we made in _____. According to whose likeness _____. So if you are created in Their image, you should see your image as beautiful. When you don't see yourself like Them, we are saying, "God, You didn't create everything beautiful." You are saying that He doesn't do everything good. What job would you say God gave us? _____ over the earth. God did what to the male and female, _____ them. He gave a command. What was it _____ and _____. We are to fill what? The _____ and _____ it.

Let's look deeper at what "subdue" means: to bring into subjection, conquer, vanquish, to overcome; to till or cultivate the (land).

Who do you think the scripture is referring to when it says, "Our image"? _____

_____

_____

_____

_____

_____

Titus 3:4–7 HCSB: "But when the goodness of God and His love for mankind appeared, He saved us, not by works of righteousness that we had done, but according to His mercy, through the washing of regeneration and by renewal by the Holy Spirit. He poured out this Spirit on us abundantly through Jesus Christ our

Savior, so having been justified by His grace, we may become heirs with the hope of eternal life."

What two characters traits of God are referred to in the beginning? _____ and _____. Who did He reveal these traits to? _____ What does He do for mankind? _____ according to His _____ Who renews us? _____. We have been justified through who? _____. We become _____ with hope of _____.

Pray this prayer with me aloud: Lord, I am honored to be created in Your image. Please forgive me for the times I don't like who I am or what I look like. How You have created me is good, very good. Holy Spirit, give me the wisdom and insight on how to change the way I view myself. Help me to gaze at the mirror of God, so I see what He sees. Give me the courage and guidance to make healthy choices in caring for my body with the food I eat and the exercise I do. I thank You, Lord, for what You have done already and what You are going to do for and in me. In Jesus's name, I pray. Amen

Example Page

Scripture

John 4:23 NIV: "But the time is coming indeed it's here now when true worshippers will worship the Father in spirit and in truth. The Father is looking for those who will worship Him in that way."

What is it about this scripture that spoke to you? That once I accepted Christ as my Lord and Savior, the Holy Spirit resides in me. The Holy Spirit connects my spirit with God's spirit, and I am now a true worshiper. I can worship in the truth. I can receive understanding and knowledge about God the Father; Jesus, His son; and the Holy Spirit. I am surround by this material world and it tries to define who I am, but the Holy Spirit is connected to my spirit, and He is defining me. I have freedom from the grasp of the world.

Do you truly believe what it says? No, I need to study it more thoroughly.

Journal Page

John 4: 22–26 AMP:

> You (Samaritan) (Tina) do not know what
> you are worshiping (you worship what you do not
> comprehend.) (we worship what we have knowl-
> edge of and understanding.) For (after all) salva-
> tion comes from(among) the Jews. A time will
> come however, indeed it is already here, when the
> true (genuine) worshipers will worship the Father
> in spirit and in truth (reality); for the Father is
> seeking just such people as these as His worship-
> ers. God is a Spirit (a Spiritual Being) and those
> who worship Him in spirit and truth. (reality)

John 4:21–25 MSG: "Believe Me, woman, (Tina) the time is
coming when you Samaritans will worship the Father neither here
at this mountain or there in Jerusalem. You worship guessing in the
dark; we Jews worship in clear light of day."

Commentary Bible in spirit and truth, in virtue of new birth,
and in light of revelation of truth in Christ. God is a spirit describes
His Sovereign Freedom. Which is in contrast to me. Men must,
therefore, worship Him in Spirit by which they can commune with
Him.

How will I apply this truth to my life? I will try to walk in the
freedom of the Spirit of truth. By allowing for quite time daily with
the Lord so the Holy Spirit can be active in my life; allowing Him to
reveal new facets of the Sovereign God to me.

Pray this prayer aloud: Father, I humbly come before You in
worship and honor of You. I thank You that Your Spirit and mine are
united and it can never be separated because I am a true worshiper
through Your Son, Jesus Christ. Thank You, Holy Spirit, for making
me alive and be one with the Father's spirit. Thank You for giving me
freedom from this sinful world. I am a true worshiper, and I worship
You in spirit and truth. In Jesus's name, I pray. Amen.

In this section, you will find five scriptures on this topic. As you pray to and seek the Holy Spirit, ask for guidance. Ask Him to reveal who God says you are. As you apply the truth, each scripture will build your knowledge and trust in God's Word. If you want to go deeper, find corresponding scriptures and look up words whose meaning you are unsure of.

Scripture

_____

_____

_____

_____

_____

_____

_____

_____

_____

What is it about this scripture that spoke to you?

_____

_____

_____

_____

_____

Do you truly believe what it says? Yes or no. Explain your answer.

_____

_____

_____

_____

_____

Journal Page

How will I apply this truth to my life?

_____
_____
_____
_____
_____
_____

Write out your prayer:

_____
_____
_____
_____
_____
_____

If the Holy Spirit has revealed a time you have lived this truth out, write it down.

_____
_____
_____
_____
_____

Scripture

_____
_____
_____
_____
_____

What is it about this scripture that spoke to you?

_____

_____

_____

_____

_____

_____

Do you truly believe what it says? Yes or no. Explain your answer.

_____

_____

_____

_____

_____

_____

Journal Page

How will I apply this truth to my life?

_____

_____

_____

_____

_____

_____

Write out your prayer:

_____

_____

_____

_____

_____

_____

If the Holy Spirit has revealed a time you have lived this truth out, write it down.

_____

_____

_____

_____

_____

_____

Scripture

_____

_____

_____

_____

_____

_____

What is it about this scripture that spoke to you?

_____

_____

_____

_____

_____

_____

Do you truly believe what it says? Yes or no. Explain your answer.

_____

_____

_____

_____

_____

_____

Journal Page

How will I apply this truth to my life?

_____

_____

_____

_____

_____

_____

Write out your prayer:

_____

_____

_____

_____

_____

_____

If the Holy Spirit has revealed a time you have lived this truth out, write it down.

_____

_____

_____

_____

_____

_____

Scripture

_____

_____

_____

_____

_____

_____

What is it about this scripture that spoke to you?

_____

_____

_____

_____

_____

_____

Do you truly believe what it says? Yes or no. Explain your answer.

_____

_____

_____

_____

_____

_____

Journal Page

How will I apply this truth to my life?

_____
_____
_____
_____
_____
_____

Write out your prayer:

_____
_____
_____
_____
_____

If the Holy Spirit has revealed a time you have lived this truth out, write it down.

_____
_____
_____
_____
_____

Scripture

_____
_____
_____
_____
_____

What is it about this scripture that spoke to you?

_____

_____

_____

_____

_____

_____

Do you truly believe what it says? Yes or no. Explain your answer.

_____

_____

_____

_____

_____

_____

Journal Page

How will I apply this truth to my life?

_____

_____

_____

_____

_____

_____

Write out your prayer:

_____

_____

_____

_____

_____

_____

If the Holy Spirit has revealed a time you have lived this truth out, write it down.

_____

_____

_____

_____

_____

_____

Section 3

God Declares Who He Is

I Am the Lord your Holy One, Israel's Creator and King.

—Isaiah 43:15 NKJ

There is a lot of talk about gods, but do we really understand who the true God really is? Do we know the God who created everything we see, even the things we can't see? Do we know the God who is in complete control of everything in this world, including our lives? Do we know that God is for us and not against us? Do we know the God who gives us His best? Do you know the God of love? Do we know the God of justice, the God who heals, the God of mercy and grace? While these are just a few attributes of the one true God, His attributes are endless and worth getting to know. So let us dig deep into this chapter and discover who the God of Abraham, Isaac, and Jacob truly is

Exodus 3:6 NKJV: "Moreover He said, I am the God of thy father, the God of Abraham, the God of Isaac, and the God of Jacob. And Moses hid his face; for he was afraid to look upon God."

Colossians 1:16 NLT: "For through Him God created everything in the heavenly and on earth. He made the things we can see and the things we can't see such as thrones, kingdoms, rulers, and authorities in the unseen world. Everything was created through Him for Him."

Who is being declared as the Creator_____? What did He create_____? Things we _____ and can't _____. _____ was made for _____

We have to ask ourselves, is this true? Do we believe what it says here in the passage of scripture? If you can't say you believe, ask yourself, why don't I believe? If you want to believe and are unsure, pray to God for help with your unbelief like the father who had a son who was possessed.

Mark 9:21–25 NIV:

> Jesus asked the boy's father, "How long has he been like this?" "From childhood," he answered. "It has often thrown him into fire or water to kill him. But if You can do anything, take pity on us and help us." "'If you can'?" said Jesus. "Everything is possible for one who believes." Immediately the boy's father exclaimed, "I do

believe; help me overcome my unbelief!" When Jesus saw that a crowd was running to the scene, He rebuked the impure spirit. "You deaf and mute spirit," He said, "I command you, come out of him and never enter him again."

If God did this for this father, He will do it for you also. We just need to ask and believe. Are you ready to believe and ask? This is something we all must do to develop trust. Trust is something we are born with. God places it deep inside our spirit beings. As we grow up and face the challenges life throws at us, we lose our ability to fully trust. We allow doubts to come into our life. We become sceptics of others and of God. Before we continue on, let's pray together this prayer.

Pray this prayer aloud: Heavenly Father, I have had people hurt me, and through those hurts, I have had my trust tampered with. I ask You to help me to forgive those who have hurt me. Help me restore my trust in others but mostly in You, my creator. I now understand without trust I won't be able to grow in my understanding of who You are. I want to grow in my love and understanding of You. In Jesus's name, I pray.

1 Corinthians 13:11–13 MSG:

> When I was an infant at my mother's breast, I gurgled and cooed like any infant. When I grew up, I left those infant ways for good. We don't yet see things clearly. We're squinting in a fog, peering through a mist. But it won't be long before the weather clears, and the sun shines bright! We'll see it all then, see it all as clearly as God sees us, knowing Him directly just as He knows us! But for right now, until that completeness, we have three things to do to lead us toward that consummation: trust steadily in God, hope

unswervingly, love extravagantly. And the best of the three is love.

We all start as _____. When we don't _____ clearly. It won't be long and the weather _____ and the sun _____ bright! We will see it _____ as clear as God sees _____, Knowing _____ as He Knows us! Until that time, we have three things to do _____ Steadily in God, _____ unswervingly, _____ extravagantly. What is the best of these three? _____.

Let us take a deeper look at trust steadily. What does steady mean? Firm in position, fixed, stable; assured and direct; unfaltering, loyalty, and uninterrupted. Ask yourself, is my trust in God in a firm position? Fixed or stable? Is it assured and direct? Than ask, is it unfaltering, loyal, or uninterrupted? These are some deep questions to ask yourself. God knows that we are not perfect and doesn't expect us to be, but as we see in this scripture, if our trust is wavering, we won't see clearly. So when times of confusion comes, ask yourself, am I trusting God?

What is unswervingly hope? Unswervingly, in a constant and steadfast manner. Ask yourself, is my hope constant, and steady toward God? When our hope wavers toward God, it will waver toward ourselves and others. Hope is connected to trusting. If our trusting is in question, we need to ask, has something happened recently that has made me question my hope in God?

Love extravagantly. What does that look like? Extravagantly means lavishly, excessive, abundantly, richly, or profusely. This is the model of love God has for us. Do we accept His abundant love that He wants to lavish on us? His love is excessive and never runs out. Have you experienced this kind of love? His love is real and can penetrate any heart that opens up to Him. We need His love to love God, ourselves and others.

Pray this aloud: Holy Father God, You are so pure and full of goodness. I desire to know the fullness of Your love and I open my heart to You. Now come fill me with Your love, so I can pour Your love on others. I ask You to guide me daily in Your Word and keep me steady in all my ways. Help me to recognize if I waver in my trust or hope in You. In Jesus's name, I pray. Amen.

Psalm 91:1–2 NKJV: "He who dwells in the secret place of most High shall abide under the shadow of the Almighty. 2. This I will say of the Lord; 'He is my refuge my fortress; my God, in Him I trust.'"

We are to dwell in the_____. Of who? The _____. We abide under what? The _____ of who _____. What are we to do? _____. What are we to say that the Lord is my _____, my _____, my _____. What are we to do _____ In Him.

The Lord is to be your refuge, a place of rest where you can vision in your mind sitting upon His lap receiving comfort and protection in your times of troubles. Do you take time to be in His shelter in order to receive rest? Resting in the Lord is vital to Christian life. We all, at times, feel weary and worn down from trials, misfortunes, and losses in life. We can become disappointed with the way life is going and possibly lose hope.

I have experienced times of weariness and haven't taken time to be still before Him and rest in His presence. During those times, I am allowing pride to be active in my life, acting like I got this. I can do this without You, God. Boy, is that wrong thinking. I can't do anything without His help. With God, all things are possible. One of those times was when I was taking care of my dad's estate. I didn't seek God for His wisdom in order to handle the process. It was more work and stress than I thought it would be. I was doing everything I knew to do, and not get things resolved. I took time to sit in His shelter and to rest in His presence, and I sought Him for direction. He gave me insight and connected me to the right people who could help. This lessened the stress and got better result. We, at times, feel we are equipped for something, but it is always best to seek God for the best ways.

Isaiah 55:9 TLB: "For just as the heavens are higher than the earth, so My ways are Higher than your ways and My thoughts higher than your thoughts."

This is one of the steps we need to take to build trust in God. We need to declare with our mouth, "God, I will trust You to guide me. I will trust You to show me the best way to go. I will trust You to show me the best way to do something or the right people to talk to." Are you doing this step? What changes do you need to make to shifting your trust to God and stop relying on yourself?

Isaiah 57:18–19 NLT: "I have seen what they do, but I will heal them anyway! I will lead them. I will comfort those who mourn, bringing words of praise to their lips. May they have abundant peace, both near and far," says the LORD, who heals them."

Who sees what they have done? _____. What is the Lord willing to do for them? _____. He will also _____ them. He will do what for those who mourn? _____. What will be on our lips?_____. What does He want to give us? _____ peace.

This scripture speaks about God's character. He sees the sin we are living in and is willing to heal us to bring us back to Him. He desires to have a relationship with us. Do you desire a relationship with Him? He reveals to us that He wants to lead us. Are you willing to be led? He wants to give us peace, and not just a little, but peace in abundance. Are you living in abundant peace?

The key to have all these attributes active in your life is that you need to accept them and be willing to express thanksgiving to God, giving Him the credit for who you are. Give Him the glory for the talent He has equipped you with. When a healing comes, remember it was at the hand of God. Praise directed to God needs to come from your mouth. Don't pat yourself on the back, saying, "Look what I have accomplished, that is pride trying to rear its ugly head. Don't walk in pride be humble before the Lord."

Psalms 25:8–10 NLT: "The LORD is good and does what is right; He shows the proper path to those who go astray. He leads the humble in doing right, teaching them His way. The LORD leads with unfailing love and faithfulness all who keep His covenant and obey His demands."

This scripture reveals that the Lord is _____ does what is
_____. He redirects those who go _____.
We need to be_____ than He can _____ His ways.
What does He lead with _____? What is
required from you _____ His _____ and
_____ His demands.

Do you believe that the Lord is good and does what is right? There are times I don't understand why things happen as they do. For instance, I didn't understand or agree that my Mom needed to die from cancer. I was bothered by that for a long time and thought, "What is God doing? God, why didn't you heal her?" At that point in time of my life, I didn't trust God fully. I was stuck in the grieving process and felt God was absent in my life. As I cried out to Him and talked to Him about how I was feeling, God met me in my darkest hours and He brought healing to my soul and understanding to me that He was not the cause of cancer because He gives good gifts. That Satan is the thief that comes to steal, kill, and destroy life.

James 1:17 English Standard Version (ESV): "Every good gift and every perfect gift is from above, coming down from the Father of Lights, with whom there is no variation or shadow due to change."

Through the experience of my mother's cancer, it brought her and other family members into a relationship with God. They got to sense His glories' presence when she passed away. Trusting in God didn't take all the pain away from the death of my mother, but it makes it bearable. I can now reflect on our times together and have a sense of joy come over me. I am able to see death not as a complete loss but as a temporary loss because I will see her again in heaven. This brings comfort and peace to my heart and to my mind. This principle can be applied to any disappointment that occurs in life, such as losing a job, a divorce, estranged kids or family members, and so forth.

There are times when we don't understand why, but God's Word is clear; there are somethings we are to know only in part, and we get the full understanding when we get to heaven.

John 13:7 NLT: "Jesus replied, 'You don't understand now what I am doing, but someday you will.'"

That someday could be weeks, months, or years, or it will be when you get to heaven yourself. Don't let the why be your main focus. Focus on God's face and all the good He has done for you. Even if it is just the little things as I have air to breath, or I have food to cook. Or taking time to smell flowers, these are just a few examples of little things you can express thankfulness for; which will give you the strength to move forward in life with joy.

Pray this prayer aloud: Dear heavenly Father, there are times my brain cannot comprehend what is going on. I don't like the feelings it creates in me. I can become anxious, distraught, fearful, and even angry at times. I believe Your Word says we don't see things clearly, but one day, I will see as clear as You see. Your Word tells me to take shelter in You, to trust steadily in You. Your ways are higher than mine and so are Your thoughts. I declare my praises to You. You're faithful and just. You are showing me the path I should be on. You love me with unfailing love. You are the almighty God, the God of hope, and I put my hope in You right now. I ask You to lead me, to comfort me, and to put Your peace about me, to give me the understanding I need for today and tomorrow can wait. In Jesus's name, I pray. Amen.

Example

Scripture: "The LORD your God in your midst, The Mighty One, will save; He will rejoice over you with gladness, He will quiet *you* with His love, He will rejoice over you with singing."

What is it about this scripture that spoke to you? The mighty One (God) will save. That He is love, and His love will quiet me. That He is in my midst and rejoices over me.

Do you truly believe what it says? No. I am very interested first to study it out, so I can build my foundation on His love.

Journal Page

Matthew Henry's Commentary states about Zephaniah 3:17,

God will take delight in them, and do them good. The expressions of this are very lively and affecting (Zeph. 3:17): *He will rejoice over thee with joy*, will not only be well pleased with thee, upon thy repentance and reformation, and take thee into favor, but will take a complacency in thee, as the bridegroom does in his bride, or the bride in her ornaments, Isa. 62:3-5. The conversion of sinners and the consolation of saints are the joy of angels, for they are the joy of God himself. The church should be the *joy of the whole earth* (Ps. 48:2), for it is the joy of the whole heaven. He will *rest in his love*, will be *silent in his love*, so the word is. "I will not rebuke thee as I have done, for thy sins; I will acquiesce in thee, and in my relation to thee." I know not where there is the like expression of Christ's love to his church, unless in that song of songs, Song 4:9; *Thou hast ravished my heart, my sister, my spouse, with one of thy eyes.* O the condescension's of divine grace! The great God not only loves his saints, but he loves to love them, is pleased that he has pitched upon these objects of his love. He *will joy over them with singing.* He that is grieved for the sin of sinners rejoices in the graces and services of the saints and is ready to express that joy by singing over them. *The Lord takes plea-sure in those that fear him*, and in them Jesus Christ will shortly be glorified and admired.

Zephaniah describes God's victory and admiration of His redeemed people. As a victor, He will be a hero who helps, the mighty One who saves. His love will be seen as deep and felt with thoughtfulness and admiration. (He will quite you with His love.)

His satisfaction with His people will be expressed through loud, demonstrative singing. (He will rejoice over you with singing.)

Yahweh is with you. Mighty to save! His presence is one of an intimate relationship. He will give you hope during your times of battles. He will take great delight in you and quiet you with His love. We are to be silent in His love; this is so profound to me that it is inexpressible in words. We are not to struggle with the battle but let Him have it and let His love be what has the voice. In my future, I hold an intimate relationship with Yahweh, my savior. He will rejoice over me by singing.

How will I apply this truth to my life? I need to be quick to confess the sin in my life in order to ask for forgiveness. This will keep my relationship close and intimate with Jesus. By keeping this relationship with God close, He will be able to quiet me with His love, and I will have peace in my battles. I will be able to willing surrender control of my life to God, knowing that He will be rejoicing and singing over me. I will feel His presence, and this will give me the hope, trust, and strength to move forward in life.

Prayer: Most High God, I give You all my praises, and only You will I worship. You are able, willing, and desires to save me. I thank You, Lord, for You are my keeper and protector from all evil, and You keep my soul. Glories, Father of the heavens and the earth. I am grafted in Your true vine, Your son, Jesus Christ. I ask You to reveal to me any areas of my life that is not holy, not Christlike. As You reveal the sin in my life, give me the strength to lay it on Your altar, to confess them as sins against You. Give me a breakthrough in areas that hold me captive. Thank You for helping me, for believing in me, for singing over me, for giving me a future and a hope. Thank You for loving me with an endless love, a love that quiets my spirit. Help me be a witness to others of Your love, Your goodness, and Your patience. In Jesus's name, I pray. Amen.

In this section you will need to find five scriptures on this topic. As you pray and seek the Holy Spirit ask for guidance. Ask God to reveal who He is to you.

Scripture

_____
_____
_____
_____
_____

What is it about this scripture that spoke to you?

_____
_____
_____
_____
_____
_____

Do you truly believe what it says? Yes or no. Explain your answer.

_____
_____
_____
_____
_____

Journal Page

_____

_____

_____

_____

_____

_____

_____

_____

_____

_____

_____

_____

_____

_____

_____

_____

_____

_____

_____

_____

_____

_____

_____

_____

_____

_____

_____

_____

How will I apply this truth to my life?

_____

_____

_____

_____

_____

_____

Write out your prayer:

_____

_____

_____

_____

_____

If the Holy Spirit has revealed a time you have lived this truth out, write it down.

_____

_____

_____

_____

_____

_____

Scripture

_____

_____

_____

_____

_____

What is it about this scripture that spoke to you?

_____

_____

_____

_____

_____

_____

Do you truly believe what it says? Yes or no. Explain your answer.

_____

_____

_____

_____

_____

_____

Journal Page

How will I apply this truth to my life?

_____
_____
_____
_____
_____
_____

Write out your prayer:

_____
_____
_____
_____
_____
_____

If the Holy Spirit has revealed a time you have lived this truth out, write it down.

_____
_____
_____
_____
_____
_____

Scripture

_____
_____
_____
_____
_____

What is it about this scripture that spoke to you?

_____
_____
_____
_____
_____
_____

Do you truly believe what it says? Yes or no. Explain your answer.

_____
_____
_____
_____
_____
_____

Journal Page

How will I apply this truth to my life?

_____

_____

_____

_____

_____

_____

Write out your prayer:

_____

_____

_____

_____

_____

_____

If the Holy Spirit has revealed a time you have lived this truth out, write it down.

_____

_____

_____

_____

_____

_____

Scripture

_____

_____

_____

_____

_____

_____

What is it about this scripture that spoke to you?

_____

_____

_____

_____

_____

_____

Do you truly believe what it says? Yes or no. Explain your answer.

_____

_____

_____

_____

_____

_____

Journal Page

How will I apply this truth to my life?

_____
_____
_____
_____
_____
_____

Write out your prayer:

_____
_____
_____
_____
_____
_____

If the Holy Spirit has revealed a time you have lived this truth out, write it down.

_____
_____
_____
_____
_____
_____

Scripture

_____
_____
_____
_____
_____

What is it about this scripture that spoke to you?

_____
_____
_____
_____
_____
_____

Do you truly believe what it says? Yes or no. Explain your answer.

_____
_____
_____
_____
_____
_____

Journal Page

How will I apply this truth to my life?

_____
_____
_____
_____
_____
_____

Write out your prayer:

_____
_____
_____
_____
_____
_____

If the Holy Spirit has revealed a time you have lived this truth out, write it down.

_____
_____
_____
_____
_____
_____

Section 4

God's Promises to Me

Every good thing the Lord promised them came true.

—Joshua 21:45 TLB

Let's take a deeper look at what is a promise. Webster dictionary1828.com says this:

> Promise: A binding declaration of something to be done or given for another's benefit. A *promise* may be absolute or conditional; lawful or unlawful; express or implied. An absolute *promise* must be fulfilled at all events. The obligation to fulfill a conditional *promise* depends on the performance of the condition. An unlawful *promise* is not binding, because it is void; for it is incompatible with a prior paramount obligation of obedience to the laws. An express *promise* is one expressed in words or writing. An implied *promise* is one which reason and justice dictate. Promise brings hopes; expectation, or that which affords expectation of future distinction. To make a written or spoken declaration to another, which binds the promiser in honor, conscience, or law, to do or forbear some act. To *promise* one's self, to be assured or to have strong confidence.

In scripture, the *promise* of God is the declaration or assurance which God has given in His Word of bestowing blessings on His people. Such assurance resting on the perfect justice, power, benevolence, and immutable veracity of God cannot fail in performance. The Lord is not slack concerning His promises.

Second Peter 3:8–9 TLB: "But don't forget this dear friends, that a day or a thousand years from now is like tomorrow to the Lord. He isn't really being slow about His promised return, even though it sometimes seems that way. But He is waiting, for the good reason that He is not willing that any should perish, and He is giving more time for sinners to repent."

What immutable means, Websterdictionary1828.com says is "unalterable; not capable or susceptible of change." That by two *immutable* things, in which it was impossible for God to lie, we might have strong consolation.

God is not _____ about His promises. He is waiting because He doesn't want any to _____. He is giving us time to _____.

Hebrews 6:17–20 Easy-to-Read Version (ERV):

> God wanted to prove that His promise was true. He wanted to prove this to those who would get what He promised. He wanted them to understand clearly that His purposes never change. So God said something would happen, and He proved what He said by adding an oath. These two things cannot change: God cannot lie when He says something He cannot lie! When He makes an oath. So these two things are a great help to us who have come to God for safety. They encourage us to hold on to the hope that is ours. This hope is like an anchor for us. It is strong and sure and keeps us safe. It goes behind the curtain. [d] Jesus has already entered there and opened the way for us. He has become the high priest forever, just like Melchizedek.

God proved His _____ are true. Who did He want to prove this to? _____ who gets what He promises. He wants us to know His purposes never _____. God cannot _____ when He speaks, nor can He lie when He makes an _____. What are we encouraged to hold on to_____? Hope is like what _____? Hope keeps us _____. Jesus entered behind what? _____. He became the _____.

What does veracity mean? Websterdictionary1828.com says; "Habitual observance of truth, or habitual truth; as a man of *veracity* His *veracity* is not called in question."

This information gives us a very clear picture of God's character, of how He is truth. He cannot lie. He keeps His promises to us. He is not changed or influenced by anything we do or do not do, say or do not say. This should give us great confidence and hope in Him, that when we go to Him with one of His promises in the Word of God, the Bible, with the right heart attitude of worship and honoring Him, He will answer our request with His promises to us.

Humans have the tendency of not always keeping their promises to themselves or even with others. When this happens, it brings an attitude of mistrust into our hearts. We need to learn to separate the actions and character of others from God's character. If we don't do this, we will see God as we see our fellow humans, as one that breaks His promise to us. This will bring doubt into our minds, that we can't trust God at His Word. This is very critical to our relationship with God. We need to be able to know and trust His Word. We need to learn to compare all our thoughts, motives, and actions to His Word. When we do this, it will give us the foundation needed to stand on. That foundation will be firm and immutable, which is unchangeable just like God. We will be a person of veracity; our character will not be questioned because we practice truth as God is truth.

Right now, I think we need to pray. Father God, You know who the people in my life that have made promises either verbal or written to me and have not kept them. You know the mistrust I have for them. Right now, I declare that I forgive them for not keeping their promises to me. I ask You to forgive me for letting this mistrust cause me to mistrust You. I ask You, Holy Spirit, to search my thoughts in order to reveal to me anyone else that I may need to go to and tell them I forgive them for not keeping their promise to me. I thank You for revealing this area of my heart to me. I praise You that what You have started You will finish. I ask this in Your precious Son's name, Jesus Christ. Amen.

This is very exciting. Now that we have our heart right with God, we will be able to apply some of His promises in His Word to our life. We will see our ability to discern the truth, and our trust in God grow.

Joshua 24:17 NIV: "It was the Lord our God Himself who brought us and our parents up out of Egypt, from that land of slavery, and preformed those great signs before our eyes. He protected us on our entire journey and among all the nations through which we traveled."

Who brought us and our parents out of Egypt? _____.
What did He perform before our eyes? _____.
He _____ us on our _____ journey and our travels through all _____. Let's look at what Egypt was like.

Exodus 1:11–14 NIV:

> So they put slave masters over them to oppress them with forced labor, and they built Pithom and Rameses as store cities for Pharaoh. But the more they were oppressed, the more they multiplied and spread; so, the Egyptians came to dread the Israelites and worked them ruthlessly. They made their lives bitter with harsh labor in brick and mortar and with all kinds of work in the fields; in all their harsh labor the Egyptians worked them ruthlessly.

Exodus 2:23–25 NIV: "During that long period, the king of Egypt died. The Israelites groaned in their slavery and cried out, and their cry for help because of their slavery went up to God. God heard their groaning and He remembered His covenant with Abraham, with Isaac and with Jacob. So God looked on the Israelites and was concerned about them."

Exodus 5:10–14 NIV:

> Then the slave drivers and the overseers went out and said to the people, "This is what Pharaoh says: 'I will not give you any more straw. Go and get your own straw wherever you

can find it, but your work will not be reduced at all.'" So the people scattered all over Egypt to gather stubble to use for straw. The slave drivers kept pressing them, saying, "Complete the work required of you for each day, just as when you had straw." And Pharaoh's slave drivers beat the Israelite overseers they had appointed, demanding, "Why haven't you met your quota of bricks yesterday or today, as before?"

The Israelites were oppressed, worked ruthlessly, and their lives was made bitter by the hard labor they were forced to complete daily. The slaves, were pressed, and beaten. They groaned and cried out to God.

Exodus 12:42 NIV: "Because the LORD kept vigil that night to bring them out of Egypt, on this night all the Israelites are to keep vigil to honor the LORD for the generations to come."

What is meant by "God kept vigil"? Websterdictionary1828. com states that it is "watch; devotion performed in the customary hours of rest or sleep."

Matthew Henry's Commentary states,

The ordinances of that night, in the annual return of it, were to be carefully observed: *This is that night of the Lord,* that remarkable night, to be celebrated in all generations. Note, the great things God does for His people are not to be a nine days' wonder, as we say, but the remembrance of them is to be perpetuated throughout all ages, especially the work of our redemption by Christ. This first Passover-night was a night of the Lord *much to be observed;* but the last Passover-night, in which Christ was betrayed (and in which the Passover, with the rest of the ceremonial institutions, was superseded and abolished), was a night of the Lord *much more to be observed*, when a yoke heavier than that of Egypt was broken from off our necks, and a land better than that of Canaan set before us.

That was a temporal deliverance to be celebrated *in their generation*; this is an eternal redemption to be celebrated in the praises of glorious saints, *world without end. The night of the Lord*; the First Passover; that remarkable night, when God broke the heavy yoke of slavery off of the Egyptians. Is to be celebrated in all generations to come. The last Passover-night, was a night of the Lord *much more to be observed*, this was the night when Christ broke your yoke of slavery and promised you eternity in heaven. This should be passed onto all generations to come.

Yokes of slavery that once held me are sexual abuse, lying, stealing, and gossip. The desire to be in control of everything in my life and other's choices in their life was because, I didn't understand what trust was. I dealt with thoughts of unfaithfulness. I was not satisfied in my marriage and was drawn into seeking attention from others. I Growing up with an alcoholic father I was aware that I could become a slave to abusing alcohol because, I see many of my family struggle with alcohol abuse. Watching soap operas gave me a very distorted view of what married life was to be like. Poverty was another area I came from a very large family and we didn't have much at all, so the mindset I had is I will always struggle financially. Self-hatred was one of the hardest areas I didn't like how I looked or what I felt about myself. Depression, anger, and dissatisfaction were other areas. These are areas I have overcome in my life by studying and applying the Word of God. I needed to learn to surrender control over to the Holy Spirit, to call on Him in order to give me wisdom and understanding. I needed to learn to have the Holy Spirit search my heart in order to bring conviction, and I needed to do the work of changing. Changing and breaking the yokes of slavery, it takes God's grace to have the strength and desire to overcome these. When we slip up and sin again, as we all will do at times until we go home to be with Jesus, remember what is needed to be done. We need to confess it to God, turn away from the sin, and accept God's grace.

What yokes of slavery is Jesus wanting to break off you?

_____

_____

_____

_____

_____

As you say this prayer, speak out loud each yoke of slavery (sin) that the Holy Spirit revealed to you. Pray this prayer aloud: Father God, I confess to You all the yokes of slavery _____ that are sin that have held me captive. I renounce each one of them. I thank You for delivering me from all of them. I now understand the importance of remembering the things that once held me captive, so I can share with the generations to come the goodness of my God. Holy Spirit, I ask You to search my heart to see if there are any other areas of my life that I am still in slavery, so I can confess them to God, so He can deliver me from them. In Jesus's name, I pray.

The last part of Joshua 24:17 scripture talks about how "He *protected* us on *our entire* journey and among all the nations through which we traveled."

What did God do? _____. Was this a short time? _____. How long does He protect _____ journey?

What does entire mean to you?

_____

_____

_____

_____

_____

Websterdictionary1828.com: "entire; whole; undivided; unbroken; complete in its parts. Wholly devoted; firmly adherent; faithful." The first part describes the journey, the second describes God's character toward us.

What do you think is meant by through all nations we traveled?

_____

_____

_____

_____

_____

For the Israelites, it was the physical lands they had traveled through to get to the Promised Land. I also see it as the purification process they went through when they surrendered the idols they were worshipping and the sins in their heart. The idol worshipping and sin held in their hearts which caused a separation in their relationship with God. The process of sanctification took forty years to set them free, and be delivered out of the wilderness. Some didn't make it out. Do you see how patient God is? He knows we are a work in progress. He is a gentle man and doesn't force us to do anything we are not willing to do. When we know, deep inside our heart, that there are changes, we need to make and chose not to; we are choosing to walk in rebellion against God.

Rebellion to God is sin; this action opens us up to Satan and his army. God rewards our obedience to His commands. He is standing by all the time, waiting for us to repent and seek His help. That is why this scripture talks about our entire journey. There may be times we may want to give up on God, but remember, He won't give up on you. Hold fast to His Word, to His promises; gather around you a good support of likeminded Christians who can give you the support and encouragement in times of pressure and hardship.

What are idols? For me, one was putting my friends and some of my family members before God. When problems arise, I would seek the advice of friends and family first in order to help me resolve the issue. Then one day, God asked me a simple question, "Do they have knowledge above Me?" This took me by surprise, and I got out my Bible and the Holy Spirit lead me.

Isaiah 55:8–11 MSG:

> "I don't think the way you think. The way you work isn't the way I work." GOD's Decree. "For as the sky soars high above earth, so the way I work surpasses the way you work, and the way I think is beyond the way you think. Just as rain and snow descend from the skies and don't go back until they've watered the earth, Doing their work of making things grow and blossom, producing seed for farmers and food for the hungry, So will the words that come out of My mouth not come back empty-handed. They'll do the work I sent them to do, they'll complete the assignment I gave them.

This correction God brought to my heart has helped me to trust Him more. I now have the understanding that I need to seek God first, and that He wants to be my source in my times of need. Now I'm not saying it is wrong to talk to family and friends, but we need to compare their advice to God's Word, and if it doesn't match, always take God's Word over theirs. God will never lead you astray or give you wrong advice. He loves you as much as He loves His one and only son, Jesus. God desires us. He wants more than anything to have a relationship with you.

Isaiah 54:10 AMP: "For though the mountains should depart, and the hills be shaken *or* removed, yet My love *and* kindness shall not depart from you, nor shall My covenant of peace *and* completeness be removed, says the Lord, Who has compassion on you."

What should depart? The _____. What will happen to the hills?_____ or_____.

Whose love and kindness won't depart? _____ what else

won't be removed? _____ of _____. What
does the _____ have on you _____.

Do you believe God is a God of love and kindness?
Why?

_____

_____

_____

_____

_____

Pray this prayer: Father God, You know what is inside my heart better than I do. I want to know the love You have for me in a deeper, more real way. I ask You, Holy Spirit, to search my heart and expose any areas of doubt I may have about God. I also want You to search my heart to see if there are any areas in my life where I have an idol, something I place a higher value on than God. Father God, I want to be obedient to Your Word. I love You, Father God. In the name of Jesus, I pray. Amen.

Take some time and be still in your thoughts and actions, listen to hear a word from God through the Holy Spirit. When He speaks to you, use the Bible to confirm what He said. Ask the Holy Spirit to lead you to a scripture that will confirm what was spoken. This will give you the confidence you hear from God, and it was not Satan using your flesh to speak to yourself. Find the scripture God wants you to study and learn to apply it to your life. Write this scripture out and refer to it until you have it settled in your heart.

_____

_____

_____

_____

_____

Take time to say your own prayer, using this scripture to confess to God what needs to be repented or to ask forgiveness. If you don't believe this scripture, tell Him to help you in your unbelief. Or it could be a prayer of thanksgiving for this new understanding being revealed to you. All of these steps in prayer will bring freedom, chains will be broken, and foster a deeper relationship with your Father God and His son, Jesus.

Write your prayer here, so when you feel unsettled in this area of your life, you can go back to it and say, "Satan it was finished, completed, put to rest on this day _____ you have lost."

_____
_____
_____
_____
_____
_____
_____
_____
_____
_____

Example Page

Scripture

Isaiah 50:4–5 MSG: "The Master, GOD, has given me a well-taught tongue, So I know how to encourage tired people. He wakes me up in the morning, Wakes, me up, opens my ears to listen as one ready to take orders. The Master, GOD, opened my ears, and I didn't go back to sleep, didn't pull the covers back over my head. I followed orders."

What is it about this scripture that spoke to you? That God can equip me to speak the truth of His Word to others. I can encourage others with His Word. He opens my ears to listen to Him. I have the choice to be obedient to His instructions.

Do you truly believe what it says? Yes, I believe this scripture. I know God's Word does not lie. This scripture is a depiction of Jesus and how He lived His moments on earth. He gave to us the example we are to follow in our life. I am excited God is instructing me in this way.

Matthew Henry's Commentary states these points: the Holy Spirit was upon Jesus. Divine influence of the will of the Father daily woke Him up to pray and to preach the gospel. Christ did nothing of Himself. He spoke and did what the Father instructed Him to do.

God was in constant communication with His servants, not only with Jesus but with His prophets in the Old Testament, His disciples and apostles in the New Testament. Don't take the words "morning by morning" in the narrow sense that that is the only time God spoke to Him but take them as a sense of uninterrupted, enlightening, continually whisper in His ears.

Jesus was attentive and submissive and glad to hear from His Father. He displayed great diligence in listening, persistent prayers, and undisturbed faithfulness to obedience.

He had the spirit of wisdom within Him.

What does this scripture reveal now that you have study it out? That God spoke to the prophets of the Old Testament, to Jesus, to the disciples and apostles of the New Testament, and He still speaks to me today. God whispers constantly into the ears of those who are in a relationship with Him. He wants my inner spirit to be awake to Him at all times. He wants me to be attentive to what He is speaking, to be obedient to what He is asking or instructing me to do.

How will you apply this to your life? First, I need to learn how to shut off the noise of the world around me, so I can hear clearly from God. This will take diligence on my part. Learning to be still and listening can be hard when life is constantly pulling you in every direction. So I will need to be in constant communication with God by talking with Him, asking Him question as to what His desires are for me today, then choosing to listen and to respond in obedience to what He asks of me.

Write out your prayer: Father God, I humbly come before You. I'm thankful You whisper in my ears, that You desire fellowship with me, and that You want to instruct and guide me to share Your truth with those who need to hear it. Your Word brings great comfort, and I want to share it with others. Father God, I confess I have sinned, and I ask You to forgive me for the times You have instructed me, and I chose not to be obedient to You. I didn't just let You down, but those who need to hear Your Word. I love You and I do desire to serve You. In Jesus's name, I pray. Amen.

Share a time when you have seen this promise active in your life. I have given many words of encouragement to friends and family. I can recall one form, fourteen years ago, when I was a hairdresser and I had a client that was planning to go on a mission trip and was feeling that the health issues she was dealing with would cause her not to go. I know that God was anointing me to speak into her life. I told her God would take care of her medical needs, and He wanted her to go on that trip, and in her obedience to that, she would be a blessing to many. She went on the trip and came back feeling better than when she left. She saw many miracles performed in others' lives through God's grace and healing touch. She thanked me for being bold enough to speak to her and encouraging her to be obedient to God.

More recently, I have a sister-in-law fighting a battle with cancer. I have shared with her many scriptures of encouragement with her through the prompting of the Holy Spirit. She has received what I have told her and has been lifted up and encouraged to carry on and to fight the good fight of faith.

> Mark 10:14–16: "When Jesus saw this, he was indignant. He said to them, 'Let the little children come to me, and do not hinder them, for the kingdom of God belongs to such as these. Truly I tell you, anyone who will not receive the kingdom of God like a little child will never enter it.' And He took the children in His arms, placed His hands on them and blessed them."—Mark 10:14-16.

Mark 10:14–16 is the scripture the Lord laid on my heart for my sister-in-law.

> "Marie, last Friday when John and I came to see you, the Lord gave me this scripture Mark 10:14–16. He told me He was holding you on His lap, telling you 'to rest your head on My chest and allow Me to heal and comfort you. You are my beautiful child and I have more planned for your life than this.' I have been praying over this. I wanted to tell you this last Friday but didn't get a chance to talk with you, so I thought I would share it with you through Messenger. You are a miracle in progress. I can't wait to see how God brings the goodness out of this dark situation."

Marie's Response

> "Thank you, Tina. What a beautiful scripture. I needed to hear this. Been feeling a little overwhelmed these days. You always have this beautiful way of making me feel like I have been chosen, and that everything will be OK. God truly is working though you, and I am blessed to watch Him work though you. Love you!"

Scripture

_____

_____

_____

_____

_____

_____

_____

What is it about this scripture that spoke to you?

_____

_____

_____

_____

_____

_____

_____

Do you truly believe what it says? Yes or no. Explain your answer.

_____

_____

_____

_____

_____

_____

_____

Journal Page

How will I apply this truth to my life?

_____
_____
_____
_____
_____
_____

Write out your prayer:

_____
_____
_____
_____
_____

If the Holy Spirit has revealed a time you have lived this truth out, write it down.

_____
_____
_____
_____
_____

Scripture

_____
_____
_____
_____
_____
_____

What is it about this scripture that spoke to you?

_____

_____

_____

_____

_____

_____

Do you truly believe what it says? Yes or no. Explain your answer.

_____

_____

_____

_____

_____

Journal Page

How will I apply this truth to my life?

_____
_____
_____
_____
_____

Write out your prayer:

_____
_____
_____
_____
_____

If the Holy Spirit has revealed a time you have lived this truth out, write it down.

_____
_____
_____
_____
_____

Scripture

_____
_____
_____
_____
_____

What is it about this scripture that spoke to you?

_____

_____

_____

_____

_____

_____

Do you truly believe what it says? Yes or no. Explain your answer.

_____

_____

_____

_____

_____

Journal Page

How will I apply this truth to my life?

_____
_____
_____
_____
_____
_____

Write out your prayer:

_____
_____
_____
_____
_____

If the Holy Spirit has revealed a time you have lived this truth out, write it down.

_____
_____
_____
_____

Scripture

_____
_____
_____
_____
_____
_____

What is it about this scripture that spoke to you?

_____

_____

_____

_____

_____

_____

Do you truly believe what it says? Yes or no. Explain your answer.

_____

_____

_____

_____

_____

Journal Page

How will I apply this truth to my life?

_____

_____

_____

_____

_____

_____

Write out your prayer:

_____

_____

_____

_____

_____

If the Holy Spirit has revealed a time you have lived this truth out, write it down.

_____

_____

_____

_____

_____

Scripture

_____

_____

_____

_____

_____

_____

What is it about this scripture that spoke to you?

_____

_____

_____

_____

_____

_____

Do you truly believe what it says? Yes or no. Explain your answer.

_____

_____

_____

_____

_____

Journal Page

_____
_____
_____
_____
_____
_____
_____
_____
_____
_____
_____
_____
_____
_____
_____
_____
_____
_____
_____
_____
_____
_____
_____
_____
_____
_____
_____
_____
_____
_____
_____
_____

How will I apply this truth to my life?

_____
_____
_____
_____
_____
_____

Write out your prayer:

_____
_____
_____
_____
_____

If the Holy Spirit has revealed a time you have lived this truth out, write it down.

_____
_____
_____
_____
_____

Section 5

What Jesus Did for Me

For their sake [a]I sanctify Myself [to do Your will], so that they also may be sanctified [set apart, dedicated, made holy] in [Your] truth.

—John 17:19 AMP

Jesus sanctified Himself to do His Father's will. Jesus is the example of how we are to act today. If He need to be sanctified in the truth of God's Word, how much more do we?

Let's take a deeper look it to *sanctification*: (*Encyclopedia of the Bible*) "to make holy," one of the most important concepts in the Bible. Sanctification may be defined as the process of acquiring sanctity or holiness as a result of association with deity. The objective of sanctification is purity, whether ritual or moral purity or both. Not only are there outward sins, but we deal with defilement as well. Being sanctified gives hope for inner renewal of the spirit. The spirit of truth will purge the believer's heart from all impurity and make perfect their relationship with God. A believer is now separated from the world and joined to Christ.

Psalms 19:12–13 TLB: "But how can I ever know what sins are lurking in my heart? Cleanse me from these hidden faults and keep me from deliberate wrongs; help me to stop doing them. Only then can I be free of guilt and innocent of some great crime."

What is lurking in your heart? _____ What do we need to ask for? To be _____ from hidden _____. From _____ wrongs. What will we be free of? _____. We become? _____ of great _____.

Ponder this scripture for a moment; let it soak into your heart. No one, except Christ, is exempt from sin. We all have sin lurking in our heart. We need the Holy Spirit to reveal the areas of sin to us, to bring conviction to our minds, so we can take the action needed to confess sin, walk away, and resist the temptation to sin again. We must desire to be free from sin and the guilt that comes with sin. We must be deliberate at walking away from the sin that once held us captive.

This is our part in being sanctified. We need to understand that God is the most valuable asset and the time we put into our relationship with Him is the best use of our time. We all have commitments in our lives, and we can't just stop them, but we can examine our schedules to see where we can make needed adjustments to work God in.

When I started my journey with God and His Son Jesus, I need more time in the Word. I needed to study out scripture like we are doing in this study. As my relationship grew, I came to understand that His promises I have found in the Bible are true. I needed to learn how to apply them in my life. My walk now is more like a constant conversation. His Word is on my mind, worship music is playing in the background, and I'm seeking His guidance throughout my day. When the Holy Spirit reveals to my heart an area that I am holding on to or that is causing me to stumble or that is putting a distance between me and God. I need to study this out in the Word of God, the Bible, allowing the Holy Spirit access.

This act of submission is how freedom has come in many areas of my life. I dig in deep and study it out. These are the steps I take in sanctifying myself. I build myself up through His Word, building my level of trust and growing my relationship with Him. I confess the promises from the Bible aloud, and I ponder on them throughout the day.

I apply action to what I am studying. You may wonder what action one applies? There are different actions that can be done. One is controlling your thoughts. When a wrong thought enters your mind, you need to stop thinking on that immediately and refocus your thoughts on God's Word. It could be an action you are doing, like speeding. You recognize you are speeding, so you slow down and confess to God you are sorry for sinning by breaking the laws of our state.

Psalm 24:3–6 NLT: "Who may climb the mountain of the LORD? Who may stand in His holy place? Only those whose hands and hearts are pure, who do not worship idols and never tell lies. They will receive the LORD's blessing and have a right relationship with God their savior. Such people may seek You and worship in Your presence, O God of Jacob."

What is required of us? _____ and _____ are _____. Don't _____ idols. Never _____.

When our relationship is right, what do we receive from the Lord?
_____.

The word "pure" means (Websterdictionary1823.com) "free from moral defilement; without spot; not sullied or tarnished; incorrupt; undebased by moral turpitude; holy."

Websterdictionary1823.com states; Turpi'tude, *noun* (Latin *turpitudo*, from *turpis*, foul, base).

1. Inherent baseness or vileness of principle in the human heart; extreme depravity.
2. Baseness or vileness of words or actions; shameful wickedness.

We now have a new truth that we need to process, accept, and apply in our life. The heart and hands are to be free from sin and idol worship. This scripture exposes that sin lurks in our heart. Our heart is where everything starts, so we will study the next three scriptures out and learn how to apply them to our life. I want you to read them as a prayer, putting your name in each scripture.

Pray this prayer aloud: Father God, as we read and study these scriptures, open our heart to the Holy Spirit; let His convection come over us to bring the true repentance we need. I take Your authority right now, and I bind commendation! Commendation is the work of Satan, and he has no authority over us who trust in and claim Jesus as our Lord and Savior. I pray You give us Your discernment and the strength to make the adjustments and to confess the hidden sins we have been holding captive in our hearts. Renew our strength, so we can stand firmly on Your Word, so when Satan puts a stumble block in our path, we recognize it and we can avoid it. In Jesus's name, I pray. Amen.

Proverbs 4:20–24 NLT: "My child (Name), pay attention to what I say. Listen carefully to My Words. Don't lose sight of them. Let them penetrate deep into your heart, for they bring life to (me) those who find them, and healing to (my) their whole body. Guard (my) your heart above all else, for it determines the course of (my) your life. Avoid all perverse talk; stay away from corrupt speech."

Who is speaking to you in this scripture? _____.

What is He asking us to do? _____.

What sense are we to use? Our _____. How are we to use this sense? To _____. What are we instructed not to lose? _____ of what? _____ _____. What action describes what we are to allow the Word to do? _____. What part of us is it to affect? _____. When we find the Word, what does it bring to your body? _____ and _____. What action are we to do to our heart? _____. What part of our body determines the course of our life? _____. What are we to avoid? _____ talk, _____ speech.

Wow! That scripture was packed full of life-giving truth, and it is a lot to process. Quiet yourself and ask God to look deep into your heart, asking Him:

Do I guard my heart?

_____

_____

_____

_____

Do I pay attention and listen to Your Word?

_____

_____

_____

_____

Do I speak in ways that are harmful to You, to myself, or others?

_____

_____

_____

_____

_____

Take time now to pray, thanking God for revealing His truth and showing His mercies and grace to you, so you can accept who you are, and you can repent and accept who He wants you to be.

Write in your journal what the Holy Spirit reveals to you.

_____

_____

_____

_____

_____

Psalms 139:23–24 NLT: "Search (Name) me, O *God*, and know my heart; test me and know my *anxious* thoughts. *Point out* anything in me that offends You and *lead* me along the path of everlasting *life*."

Who do we want searching and knowing our heart? _____. What kind of thoughts can we have? _____. What do we want God to do with what offends Him? _____. What do we want God to do for us? _____us on paths to everlasting _____. Take time now to pray.

Thank God for revealing His truth and showing His mercies and grace to you so you can accept who you are, and you can repent and accept who He wants you to be.

Ask Him to point out anything that offends Him.

———————————————————————————
———————————————————————————
———————————————————————————
———————————————————————————

Ask Him, "Do I have any anxious thoughts or areas where I don't trust in You?"

———————————————————————————
———————————————————————————
———————————————————————————
———————————————————————————
———————————————————————————

Psalm 51:1–10 NLT:

> Have mercy on (name) me, O God, because of Your unfailing love. Because of Your great compassion, blot out the stain of my sins. Wash me clean from my guilt. Purify me from my sin. For I (Name) recognize my rebellion; it haunts me day and night. Against You, and You alone, have I sinned; I have done what is evil in Your sight. You will be proved right in what You say, and Your judgment against (Name) me is just.[a] For I was born a sinner—yes, from the moment my mother conceived me. But You desire honesty from the womb,[b] teaching me wisdom even there. Purify me from my sins,[c] and I will be clean; wash me, and I will be whiter than snow. Oh, give me back my joy again; You have broken me—now let me rejoice. Don't keep looking at my sins. Remove the stain of my guilt. Create in me a clean heart, O God. Renew a loyal spirit within me.

We want what from God? _____. God's character is _____ and great _____.
What do we want God to do _____ out and purify
me from _____. Wash me clean of _____.
What do we need to do? Recognize my _____. Who
have we sinned against? _____. God desires me to
be? _____. When He purifies us, how do we look?
_____ than _____. We ask for Him to give
us what? _____. Now we _____. God will create in
you a clean _____ and renew a _____
spirit.

Take time now to pray. Thank God for revealing His truth and
showing His mercies and grace to you, so you can accept who you are
and you can repent and accept who He wants you to be.

Ask what sins need to be blotted out.

_____
_____
_____
_____

**Ask Him if you have a root of rebellion hiding within your
life?**

_____
_____
_____
_____

It takes God's grace to be sanctified. We need to learn how to
apply His grace and understand what grace is. So as we study the next
set of scriptures, take your time and ponder on them.

Romans 6:1–3 TPT: "So what do we do, then? Do we persist
in sin so that God's kindness and grace will increase? What a terrible

thought! We have died to sin once and for all, as a dead man passes away from this life. So how could we live under sin's rule a moment longer? Or have you forgotten that all of us who were immersed into union with Jesus, the Anointed One, were immersed into union with His death?"

What are we not to persist in? _____ When does our death to sin occur? When we _____ into a _____ with who? _____ the _____. Immerse in union with Jesus Christ in the union of? _____.

Romans 6:6–11 TLB:

> Your old evil desires were nailed to the cross with Him; that part of you that loves to sin was crushed and fatally wounded, so that your sin-loving body is no longer under sin's control, no longer needs to be a slave to sin; for when you are deadened to sin you are freed from all its allure and its power over you. And since your old sin-loving nature "died" with Christ, we know that you will share His new life. Christ rose from the dead and will never die again. Death no longer has any power over Him. He died once for all to end sin's power, but now He lives forever in unbroken fellowship with God. So look upon your old sin nature as dead and unresponsive to sin, and instead be alive to God, alert to Him, through Jesus Christ our Lord.

What was nailed to the cross with Christ? _____ _____. The part of you that sinned was _____ and _____. Sin can no longer _____ you. You will no longer be a _____ to sin. Christ was raised from what? _____. Why did He die? To end _____ we are to be alive to _____ fellowship with who?

_____ Through who? _____ our

_____.

Romans 6:12–16

> Do not let sin control the way you live;[a] do not give in to sinful desires. Do not let any part of your body become an instrument of evil to serve sin. Instead, give yourselves completely to God, for you were dead, but now you have new life. So, use your whole body as an instrument to do what is right for the glory of God. Sin is no longer your master, for you no longer live under the requirements of the law. Instead, you live under the freedom of God's grace. Well then, since God's grace has set us free from the law, does that mean we can go on sinning? Of course not! Don't you realize that you become the slave of whatever you choose to obey? You can be a slave to sin, which leads to death, or you can choose to obey God, which leads to righteous living.

How do you see the words "do not" as a suggestion or a command? _____. Yes, they are a command and should be treated with respect by honoring God. Obeying His commands is how we show Him honor and show Him that we love and trust Him. What are we not to obey? _____. Sin is not to_____our life. What are we not to give into_____. How are we to give ourselves? _____. What are we to use as an instrument? Our _____ body. We are to use our body by doing what is _____ to give God _____. Our master is no longer what? _____. We live under God's freedom of what? _____. We become a slave to what we choose to _____. Obeying God leads us to _____living.

When you are in the right standing with God. We are not perfect, and that is why we have the Holy Spirit. He will help guide us into choosing to live with and for God. He will steer us clear from living a life of habitual sin, which brings death. When He reveals an area of sin to you, receive His correction, embrace it. Seek for truth in God's Word where the truth can be found. We can be set free from the grips of sin. This is an action we need to do all day long. We need to evaluate: are we obeying God in this moment? We can be guided and led into righteous living and never live a life of sinful desires. This takes a deep commitment, of being intentional in all you do. It will not be easy at first but can be done with God's grace and us applying His Word to our lives. I know you can do this; don't get discouraged. Don't allow commendation come over you, saying, "You will fail." Know that we all fail at times, and in our failures, we grow. We just need to be willing to recognize the conviction of God, saying, "I need to make an adjustment in my life." You will change and grow in this over time. God loves us so much, and He knows the challenges we face, and He has a plan and a future for us. He has laid a well-constructed path for you and me to follow. He knew, before we were created, that we would need a guide. We need to trust Him fully and rely on Him completely, intentionally seeking His wisdom.

Example Page

Romans 6:22–23 LNT: "But now you are free from the power of sin and have become slaves of God. Now you do those things that lead to holiness and result in eternal life. For the wages of sin is death, but the free gift of God is eternal life through Christ Jesus our Lord."

What is it about this scripture that spoke to you? It is telling me I must choose to trust God, that I must evaluate my actions and be aware of the choices I am making. I need to choose to live holy. I'm no longer a slave to the way I used to live; the old person is dead, and Jesus Christ paid the penalties for my sin. I now have eternal life with God for eternity.

Do you truly believe what it says? Yes, I do, but I understand this is a daily walk, and I cannot let pride in by thinking I can do it on my own.

Journal Page

Matthew Henry's Commentary states that (my paraphrase) we must choose to be dead to sin, no longer obeying it, observing it, or giving it attention. We are not to regard sin, giving it value or respect. We are to no longer fulfill its will. We are to reject our former ways. When we are dead to sin, we will see a change in our actions in all these areas of life such as; the conversations we have with people. Our work ethics at our place of business we are employed. The activities we find enjoyments in. We are changed into a true disciple. When we put to death our sinful habits and these changes bring sanctification in our heart and makes a mighty change; such a change as sanctification makes in the soul. It cuts off all correspondence with sin.

"Newness of life supposes newness of heart, for out of the heart are the issues of life. Walking, in scripture, is put for the course of the conversation, which must be new. Walk by new rules, toward new ends, from new principles. Make a new choice of the way. Choose new paths to walk in, new leaders to walk after, new companions to walk with. Old things should pass away, and all things become new" (*Matthew Henry's Commentary*).

It is to be *alive unto God through Jesus Christ our Lord*, to converse with God, to have a respect and honor toward Him, a delight in Him, a concern for Him, the soul, on all occasions, surrender toward Him to be agreeable to Him. This is how we are alive to God. The love of God reigning in the heart is the life of the soul toward God. We must choose to remove sins from the life so that we may rise again to a new life of faith and love, to never return to it, nor to have any more fellowship with the works of darkness.

Mathew Henry's Commentary on <u>Roman 6:4</u> states,

A life devoted to God is a new life; before, we were living for our self not regarding God, choosing our own way not depending on God. Now with our eyes ever toward Him, making Him the center of all our actions. *Sin shall not have dominion.* God's promises to us are more powerful and effectual for the restraining of sin than our promises to God. Sin may struggle in a believer, and may create him a great deal of trouble, but it shall not have dominion; it may vex him but shall not rule over him. *For we are not under the law, but under grace,* not under the law of sin and death, but under the law of the spirit of life, which is in Christ Jesus but under the covenant of grace, which accepts sincerity as our gospel perfection, which requires nothing but what it promises strength to perform, which is herein well ordered, that every transgression in the covenant does not put us out of covenant, and especially that it does not leave our salvation in our own keeping, but lays it up in the hands of the Mediator, who undertakes for us that sin shall not have dominion over us, who hath himself condemned it, and will destroy it; so that, if we pursue the victory, we shall come off more than conquerors but we are under grace, grace which accepts the willing mind, which is not extreme to mark what we do amiss, which leaves room for repentance, which promises pardon upon repentance; and what can be to an ingenuous mind a stronger motive than this to have nothing to do with sin? Sinners are voluntary in the service of sin. The devil could not force them into the service, if they did not yield themselves to it. This will justify God in the ruin of sinners, that they sold themselves to work wickedness: it was their own act and deed. *To iniquity unto iniquity.* Every sinful act strengthens and confirms the sinful habit: to iniquity as the work unto iniquity as the wages. Sow the wind, and reap the whirlwind; growing worse and worse, more and more hardened. The gospel is the great rule both of truth and holiness; it is the stamp, grace is the impression of that stamp; it is the form of healing words, 1 Tim. 1:13. *Secondly*, the nature of grace, as it is our conformity to that rule. 1. It is to *obey from the heart.* The gospel is a doctrine not only to be believed, but to be obeyed, and that from the heart, which denotes the sincerity and reality of that obedience; not in profession only, but in power—from the heart, the innermost part, the commanding part of us. 2. It is to be *delivered into it*, as into a mold, as the wax is cast into the impression of the seal, answering it line for line, stroke for stroke, and wholly representing the shape and figure of it. For me to be a Christian indeed is to be transformed into the likeness and similitude of the gospel, our souls answering to it, complying with it, conformed to it—understanding, will, affections, aims, principles, actions, all according to that form of doctrine.

[2.] *Being made free from sin, you became servants of* We cannot be made the servants of God till we are freed from the power and dominion of sin; we cannot serve two masters so directly opposite one to another as God and sin are. We must, with the prodigal, quit the drudgery of the citizen of the country, before we can come to our Father's house. *The gift of God is eternal life.* Heaven is life, consisting in the vision and fruition of God; and it is eternal life, no infirmities attending it, no death to put a period to it. This is the gift of God. The death is the wages of sin, it comes by desert; but the life is a gift, it comes by favor. Sinners merit hell, but saints do not merit heaven. There is no proportion between the glory of heaven and our obedience; we must thank God, and not ourselves, if ever we get to heaven. And this gift is *through Jesus Christ our Lord*. It is Christ that purchased it, prepared it, prepares us for it, preserves us to it; He is *the Alpha and Omega*, All in all in our salvation. a conscious and deliberate departure from the known will of God, then he may embrace promises which offer entire sanctification as a gift of grace.

Colossians 1:21–23 NLT:

> This includes you who were once far away from God. You were His enemies, separated from Him by your evil thoughts and actions. Yet now He has reconciled you to Himself through the death of Christ in His physical body. As a result, He has brought you into His own presence, and you are holy and blameless as you stand before Him without a single fault. But you must continue to believe this truth and stand firmly in it. Don't drift away from the assurance you received when you heard the Good News. The Good News has been preached all over the world, and I, Paul, have been appointed as God's servant to proclaim it.

Galatians 2:20–21 NLT: "My old self has been crucified with Christ. It is no longer I who live, but Christ lives in me. So, I live in this earthly body by trusting in the Son of God, who loved me and gave Himself for me. I do not treat the grace of God as meaningless. For if keeping the law could make us right with God, then there was no need for Christ to die."

Matthew Henry's Commentary states,

> Synonyms of sanctification are consecration, dedication, holiness, perfection, and separation.
>
> The process begins when one is "risen with Christ" in the new birth. Paul's emphasis on faith blends well with this emphasis upon a stage in the Christian's life when he recognizes his inner defilement, deliberately renounces a self-centeredness, and embraces by faith God's provision in Christ for full deliverance and perfection in love a conscious and deliberate departure from the known will of God, then he may embrace promises which offer entire sanctification as a gift of grace Sanctification, defined broadly as the work of God's grace in man's perfection in righteousness, begins when he becomes a believer and hence is "in Christ." It continues progressively until death brings him into Christ's presence unless he "does despite to the Spirit of grace."
>
> Parallel to the work of sanctification is the infilling of the Holy Spirit in the believer, perfection in love,

What does this scripture reveal now that you have study it out? That I cannot give any attention to sin. I need to cut off all correspondence with sin. Whatever I give my attention to will have the right to control me. I am under grace, grace which accepts the willing mind. The gospel is the great rule both of truth and holiness. The nature of grace is an act of obedience of heart. To be a Christian is to be transformed into the likeness of Christ, our souls answering to Him, complying to His commands and His will according to the doctrine written in the Bible. Grace is a free gift and when I receive His grace it will transform my life. I will be perfected in God's love.

How will you apply this to your life? I will need to daily examine my actions, asking myself, "Am I doing this onto God to bring

Him glory? Am I trusting Him in my daily living events?" I will need to have an attitude of gratitude and be able to thank God for the small and the big events, for the valleys and the mountaintop experiences. I will need to live one day at a time and not be longing for what tomorrow will bring.

Write out your prayer: Father God, I come to You with a surrender heart. I want to thank You for setting me free from sin through Your free gift of salvation through Your son, Jesus Christ. I ask You, Holy Spirit, to have Your way in my heart examine it daily, revealing to me anything that does not line up with the Word of God and with the character of Jesus. Pour Your grace over me in order to equip me to walk my life here on earth. In Jesus's name. Amen.

Share a time when you have seen this promise active in your life: The one that brought the biggest change in my heart was when I was always trying to correct my husband, John, while acting as his personal Holy Spirit. I was trying to be God and judging his actions, his words. Boy, that was so wrong to do. My actions were saying, "God, I don't trust You will do a work in John." I was dishonoring God. My actions and responses to John were not building him up. I was tearing him down. I was causing condemnation to come over him instead of God's grace and forgiveness. Once the Holy Spirit revealed this to me, I repented and asked John to forgive me. Was this easy to do? No. I had to walk in this and say daily, "God, I put John into Your hands. I will trust You God to do the work that is need in John." Sometimes, I have picked John back up, and the Holy Spirit reminds me. The impact this has had on John's life is impressive. The work God has done in John's life is way better than I could have ever imagine. He is turning into the man of God that God wants him to be. He surrendered to Christ; is faithful, kinder; and has a servant's heart. He selflessly loves me and our family. Yes, he is a work in progress. He is still surrendering areas over to God, and so am I. I will not be completed till I step foot in eternity with God the Father and His Son, Jesus Christ.

In this section, you will need to find five scriptures on this topic. As you pray and seek the Holy Spirit, ask for guidance. Ask God to reveal who He is to you.

Scripture

_____

_____

_____

_____

What is it about this scripture that spoke to you?

_____

_____

_____

_____

Do you truly believe what it says? Yes or no. Explain your answer.

_____

_____

_____

_____

_____

Journal Page

How will I apply this truth to my life?

_____

_____

_____

_____

_____

_____

Write out your prayer:

_____

_____

_____

_____

_____

If the Holy Spirit has revealed a time you have lived this truth out, write it down.

_____

_____

_____

_____

_____

Scripture

_____

_____

_____

_____

_____

What is it about this scripture that spoke to you?

_____

_____

_____

_____

_____

_____

Do you truly believe what it says? Yes or no. **Explain your answer.**

_____

_____

_____

_____

_____

Journal Page

How will I apply this truth to my life?

_____
_____
_____
_____
_____
_____

Write out your prayer:

_____
_____
_____
_____
_____
_____

If the Holy Spirit has revealed a time you have lived this truth out, write it down.

_____
_____
_____
_____
_____
_____

Scripture

_____
_____
_____
_____
_____

What is it about this scripture that spoke to you?

_____

_____

_____

_____

_____

_____

Do you truly believe what it says? Yes or no. **Explain your answer.**

_____

_____

_____

_____

_____

Journal Page

How will I apply this truth to my life?

_____
_____
_____
_____
_____
_____

Write out your prayer:

_____
_____
_____
_____
_____
_____

If the Holy Spirit has revealed a time you have lived this truth out, write it down.

_____
_____
_____
_____
_____
_____

Scripture

_____
_____
_____
_____
_____

What is it about this scripture that spoke to you?

_____

_____

_____

_____

_____

_____

Do you truly believe what it says? Yes or no. **Explain your answer.**

_____

_____

_____

_____

_____

Journal Page

How will I apply this truth to my life?

_____
_____
_____
_____
_____
_____

Write out your prayer:

_____
_____
_____
_____
_____

If the Holy Spirit has revealed a time you have lived this truth out, write it down.

_____
_____
_____
_____
_____

Scripture

_____
_____
_____
_____
_____

What is it about this scripture that spoke to you?

_____

_____

_____

_____

_____

_____

Do you truly believe what it says? Yes or no. **Explain your answer.**

_____

_____

_____

_____

_____

Journal Page

How will I apply this truth to my life?

_____

_____

_____

_____

_____

_____

Write out your prayer:

_____

_____

_____

_____

_____

_____

If the Holy Spirit has revealed a time you have lived this truth out, write it down.

_____

_____

_____

_____

_____

_____

Section 6

Answers to Questions

Section 1

What attitude is active within her? *Pride.* She won't *listen.* She *refuses* all *corrections.* She does not *trust* who *the Lord* is. She won't *seek* for *God.*

If we *listen* to the *voice* of the Lord, what do we need to do? *Obey* and do what is *right.* What will the Lord do for you? I won't make you *suffer* the *diseases.* He wants to *heal* you.

What are we to give to the Lord? *Thanks.* Who shall hear His voice? *All.*

What do we get hints of His *power?* We can hear only the *whispers.* He can be loud and thundering.

What does God's voice do from the clouds? *Echoes.* Who thunders through the sky? *"God* of *glory."* His voice can be a cry from the wilderness when we are lost and *wandering* in our ways.

Who was the voice shouting? *John.* Where was he shouting from? *Barren wilderness.* What was he asking for us to do? *Prepare* a *road.* Who are we to prepare it for? *The Lord.* What are we to do with the path? *Widen.*

How did God present himself? As a mountain *ablaze* with *fire.* What had He shown? His *glory* and His *majesty.* What did the people express? We *heard* His *voice.* What did the living God do with His people? He *spoke* to them. What did the people ask Moses to do on their behalf? Go *near* and *listen* to all. What were the people willing to do? *Listen* and *obey.*

What are we to do? *Build* yourself *up.* How? With *holy faith.* Who is the guide? The *Holy Spirit.*

155

Where did the voice come from? *Heaven.* Whose voice was it? *God's.* Who speaks truthfully? The *Holy Spirit.* Where does that voice reside? *Our heart.* How many witnesses? *Two.* To whom do the two voices belong? *God's* and the *Holy Spirit's* from *heaven.* Who were the voices witnessing about? *Jesus Christ?*

Who comes? The *Spirit* of *Truth.* What does He do? *Guides* us in all *truth?* Whose message does He give? *The Father's* He declares our *future.*

What did we receive? The *Spirit.* This spirit doesn't make us *slaves* or to live in *fear.* We are *adopted* into *sonship.* We are children of *God.*

What does good earth represent? *Hearing* the *word.* What is our responsibility? *Embrace* it. When we do our part what happens? *Produces* a *harvest.*

Who Made Humans? *God.* Whose image are we made in? *God's.* Whose nature are we to reflect? *God's.* Why are we here? *Bear fruit,* reproduce, lavish life on earth and *live bountifully!*

Section 2

God knew us before we were formed in our mother's *womb.* He *sanctified* us and *appointed* us to be a *spokesman* to the world.

Who made the heavens, the earth, the sea, and everything in them? *God.*

What does this scripture declare you are? *The temple.*

Who resides in you? *God.* God's temple is *sacred.* We are the temple of God.

We are to come and do what? *Worship* and *bow* before Him.

Who made us? *God.* We declare that *He* is our *God.* What does He do for us? *Pastures* the flock and *feeds* us.

What does the Lord of hosts declare they shall be? *Mine.* He will *publicly* recognize and openly *declare* them as His. *Jewels, My possessions,* my *treasure.* He will *spare* those who serve Him.

Who are we to watch? *God.* Then we *do* it. What mostly does God do *love you.* How are we to learn what God does? *Keep company* with Him. Who are we to observe? *Christ* How is Christ's love described? *Extravagant* He didn't love to get *something* but to give *everything* of Himself to us. We are called to *love* like that.

Who created man? *God.* In whose image are we made in? *Theirs.* According to whose likeness? *Theirs.* What job would you say God gave us? *Rule* over the earth. God did what to the male and female, *created* them. He gave a command. What was it? *Be fruitful* and *multiply.* We are to fill what? The *earth* and *subdue* it.

What two character traits of God are referred to in the beginning? *Goodness* and *love.* Who did He reveal these traits to? *Mankind.* What does He do for mankind? *Saves* according to His *mercy.* Who renews us? *The Holy Spirit.* We have been justified through who? *Jesus Christ.* We become *heirs* with hope of *eternal life.*

Section 3

Who is being declared as creator? *God.* What did He create? *Everything.* Things we *see* and can't *see. Everything* was made for *Him.*

We all start as *infants.* When we don't *see* clearly. It won't be long, and the weather *clears,* and the sun *shines* brightly! We will see it *all,* as clear as God sees *us.* Knowing *Him* as He knows us! Until that time, we have three things to *trust* steadily in God, *hope* unswervingly, *love* extravagantly. What is the best of these three? *Love.*

We are to dwell in the *secret place.* Of who? The *Most High.* We abide under what? The *shadow* of who? The *Almighty.*

What are we to do? *Say.* What are we to say that the Lord is my *refuge* my *fortress,* my *God.* What are we to do to *trust* in Him

Who see what they have done? *The Lord.*

What is the Lord willing to do for them? *Heal.* He will also *lead* them. He will do what for those who mourn? *Comfort.*

What will be on our lips? *Praise* what does He want to give us *Abundant* peace.

This scripture reveals The Lord is *good* does what is *right.* He redirects those who go *astray.* We need to be *humble* than He can *teach* His ways. What does He lead us with *unfailing love* and *faithfulness* What is required from you *keep* His *covenant* and *obey* His demands.

Section 4

God is not *slow* about His promises. He is waiting because He doesn't want any to *perish*. He is giving us time to *repent*.

God proved His *promises* are true. Who did He want to prove this to? To *those* who get what He promises are. He wants us to know that His purposes never *changed*. God cannot *lie* when He speaks, nor can He lie when He makes an *oath*. What are we encouraged to hold on to? *Hope*. Hope is like what An *anchor*. Hope keeps us *safe*. Jesus entered behind what? The *curtain*. He became the *high priest*.

Who brought us and our parents out of Egypt? *Lord, our God*. What did He *perform* before our eyes? *Great signs*. He *protects* us *throughout* our *entire* journey and our travels through all *nations*.

What did God do? *Protects* was this a short time? *No*. How long does He protect *our entire* journey?

What should depart? The *mountains*. What will happen to the hills? *Shaken* or *removed*.

Whose love and kindness won't depart? *God's*. What else won't be removed? The *covenant* of *peace*.

What does the Lord have for you? *Compassion*.

Section 5

What is lurking in your heart? *Sin*. What do we need to ask for? To be *cleansed* from hidden *faults*. From *deliberate* sins. What will we be free of? *Guilt*. We become? *Innocent* of great *crime*.

What is required of us? *Hands* and *heart* that are *pure*. Don't *worship* idols. Never *tell lies*. When our relationship is right what do we receive from the Lord? *Blessings*.

Who is speaking to you in this scripture? *God*. What is He asking us to do? To *pay attention*. What sense are we to use? Our *hearing*. How are we to use the senses for? To *listen carefully*. What are we instructed not to lose? *Sight*. Of what? *The word of God*. What action word describes what we are to allow the Word to do? *Penetrate*. What part of us is it to affect? The *heart*. When we find the Word, what does it bring to your body? *Life* and *healing*. What action are we to do to our heart? *Guard.* What part of our body determines the course of our life? *The heart.* What are we to avoid? *Perverse* talk, *corrupt* speech.

Who do we want to search and know our heart? *God.* What kind of thoughts can we have? *Anxious.* What do we want God to do with what offends Him? *Point out.* What do we want God to do for us? *Lead* us on paths to everlasting *life.*

We want what from God? *Mercy.* God's character is *unfailing love* and great *compassion.* What do we want God to do? *Blot* out and purify me from *sin.* Wash me clean of *guilt.* What do we need to do? Recognize my *rebellion.* Who have we sinned against? *God.* God desires me to be? *Honest.* When He purifies us, how do we look? *Whiter* than *snow.* We ask for Him to give us what? *Joy.* Now we *rejoice.* God will create in you a clean *heart* and renew a *loyal* spirit.

What are we not to persist in? *Sin.* When does our death to sin occur? When we are *immersed* into a *union* with who? *Jesus,* the *anointed one.* Immersed in union with Jesus Christ in the union of what? *His death.*

What was nailed to the cross with Christ? *Old evil desires.* The part of you that sinned was *crushed* and was *fatally* wounded. Sin can no longer *control* you. We will no longer be a *slave* to sin. Christ was raised from what? *The dead.* Why did He die? To end *sin's control.* We are to be alive to *unbroken* fellowship with who *God.* Through who? *Jesus Christ,* our *Lord.*

How do you see the words "do not," as a suggestion or as a command? *A command.* They are a command and should be treated with respect by honoring God. Obeying His commands is how we show Him honor and show that we love and trust Him. What are we not to obey? *Sins.* Sin is not to *control* our life. What are we not to give into? *Sinful desires.* How are we to give ourselves? *Completely.* What are we to use as an instrument? Our *whole* body. What are we to use our body by doing what is *right* to give God? *Glory.* Our master is no longer what? *Sin.* We live under God's freedom of what? *Grace.* We become a slave to what we choose to *obey.* Obeying God leads us to *righteous* living.

ABOUT THE AUTHOR

 Tina married John Young in 1987. They have two boys, Kevin and Alex. They are learning to enjoy the empty-nest season of life. Tina has had many opportunities to deepen her faith with the death of their son Kevin in 2011, and all the trials she has had to endure and overcame in her life's journey. She learned, through God guiding her, to study and apply the Word of God to her life in order to build her faith and trust in God. She loves to share with others how to develop their faith. Tina loves to study and lead Bible studies. She enjoys spending time with her family, vacationing, fishing, and playing games. Tina likes to paint pictures when she finds the time. Tina and John also enjoy hosting exchange students. They love sharing their passion for life and Jesus with them. Tina is a certified Joy Restoration Coach, certified by the Professional Christian Coaching and Counseling Academy (PCCA). She coaches those who are stuck in grief. She walks alongside friends and encourages them through their struggles in the different seasons of their life. Tina is a public speaker for Stonecroft Ministries. She travels throughout Minnesota, North and South Dakota, and Wisconsin speaking at Christian Women's Connection groups. Tina loves working part-time for the Lutheran Social Services as a direct support person. She supports people with disabilities, helping them achieve independence and accomplishing goals.